Easy-Prep Lessons

It's a Snap!

Fun Faith-Builders

David C Cook

transforming lives together

IT'S A SNAP!
Published by David C. Cook
4050 Lee Vance View
Colorado Springs, CO 80918 USA

David C. Cook Distribution Canada
55 Woodslee Avenue, Paris, Ontario, Canada N3L 3E5

David C. Cook U.K., Kingsway Communications
Eastbourne, East Sussex BN23 6NT, England

David C. Cook and the graphic circle C logo
are registered trademarks of Cook Communications Ministries.

Written by Jodi Hoch
Cover Design: BMB Design
Cover Photos: © Gaylon Wampler Photography
Interior Design: Sandy Flewelling
Illustrations: Kris & Sharon Cartwright

Scripture taken from the Holy Bible, NEW INTERNATIONAL READER'S VERSION®.
Copyright © 1996, 1998 International Bible Society. All rights reserved throughout the world.
Used by permission of International Bible Society.

ISBN 978-0-7814-4884-0

First Printing 2008
Printed in the United States

1 2 3 4 5 6 7 8 9 10

transforming lives together

Table of Contents

Introduction

Loud voices … high energy … lots of questions … occasional tears … bumps and bruises … squeals and giggle … welcome to the world of young children. They are fun-loving, and God has instilled in them a sense of adventure and wonder. As their teacher, you have been given the opportunity, the privilege, and the challenge to make an eternal impression on the lives of the children you teach. So where do you begin? Don't worry–you've grabbed the right book, *It's a Snap!*

As quick as 1 … 2 … 3 … , *It's a Snap!* will provide you with 13 delightful lessons packed with activities to engage your little ones in fun, creative and meaningful learning. Each lesson is designed for flexibility. One lesson could be completed in one hour or could be stretched out over a longer period of time, depending on the activities you choose. Remember children love and learn from lots of repetition. Each lesson is designed for grouping flexibility and personal teaching preferences. *It's a Snap!* lessons contain ideas for large groups, small groups, individuals or activity stations to suit your classroom needs.

It's a Snap! contains Bible stories where children are engaged in the actual telling of the Bible story. A *Hold'em-Up* reproducible page is provided to give the children a hands-on creation of their own. During the lesson they will have to *Hold'em-Up* to help in telling the Bible story.

We know that *Home Connections* strengthen learning when they reflect what has been learned in a classroom. *It's a Snap!* uses materials within a lesson that are commonly found in a home. This way, when the child sees at home what was used in class, such as a cotton ball, a home connection is made to the Bible story. *Home Connections* is a reproducible page with information about the lesson for the parent. It gives parents simple at-home activities that have been used in the lesson.

It's a Snap! will equip you in many ways to meet the needs of the children in your classroom. It'll be a snap to teach your little ones and to see the awe and wonder that is sparked in them as they learn about God.

Welcome to the adventure!

How to Prepare a Lesson: It's a Snap!

It's a Snap! has been designed for flexibility. Listed here are the basic parts of the lesson. You can mix and match and create your own lessons based on your preferences, the time frames you have to work within, the number of helpers you have and the needs of your classroom. Just copy and clip them together. It's a snap!

Lesson Snapshot: This chart shows all the items you will need to get for each activity.

Hold'em-Up: Use the reproducible page and the items listed to help the children create their *Hold'em-Ups*. These *Hold'em-Ups* are used during the Bible Story Time, so they must be completed **before** that time.

Round'em-Up: There are four *Round'em-Up* activities for each lesson: a Bible story connection, a song or finger play, a game and a show-me activity. These can be used **anytime** throughout the lesson as a way to round up or gather the children into group activities.

Bible Story Hands-on Activities: There are four activities for each lesson: a construction, a manipulative, a Bible Memory, and a snack activity. You may choose to do these activities **anytime** during the lesson. If you choose to do these before the Bible story, the activities lay a foundation of experiences. If done after the Bible story, they reinforce concepts taught in the Bible story.

Send'em-Off: There are three *Send'em-Off* activities: a prayer, an idea for cleanup time, and a homeward-bound activity. These activities are used after Bible Story Time and just before the children leave.

Home Connections: This is a reproducible for parents that you send home with the children. If you use the material from one lesson over a two- or three-week period, send it home the last day of your lesson.

Setting Up Your Classroom

You can create a wonderful environment that invites children to learn, celebrate and worship God. *It's a Snap!* When creating your classroom environment, keep in mind several core concepts that will foster terrific teaching and active learning.

Specialized areas

Designate several different areas within the classroom. Here are a few suggestions.

* **Construction:** Space where children can use blocks and building materials.
* **Art/Crafts:** Tables should be available for work areas for art, crafts and other tabletop activities.
* **Drama:** A drama area where children can enter into the world of pretend.
* **Large Motor:** A large open space designated for motor skills and large-group activities.
* **Quiet:** An area where children can snuggle up with a pillow or blanket and where there is little outside stimulus.
* **Small Group:** An area with designated seats, perhaps marked with an X, or spots on a special carpet.

Safety and Health

Keep in mind the safety of the children.

* Be alert for safety hazards such as broken toys or small items that could be choking hazards.
* Regularly clean toys and tabletops.
* Be aware of any health needs of the children.
* Have a system to sign children in and out and be sure to have a way to contact parents should you need them.

Celebrations

Children love to celebrate, so decorate the room and have fun. The following lessons can enhance these commonly celebrated traditions.

* National Day of Prayer: Pile on the Prayer—Lesson 5
* Christmas: Joy, Joy, Joy—Lesson 6
* Valentine's Day: God Is Full of Love—Lesson 8
* Thanksgiving: A Thankful Heart—Lesson 9
* Easter: The Butterfly in the Garden—Lesson 13

Supplies

Handy items to have in your classroom:

* **Masking Tape:** Use tape to designate areas and boundaries.
* **Storage Bags:** Place items needed for activities in zip-top bags making for easy storage and easy access during the lesson.
* **Envelopes or file folders:** Use large envelopes or file folders to store the children's completed projects until parents come to pick up the children.

More Tips for Teachers

Here are a few suggestions to make things go smoothly while you are working with your class.

Set Routines

Most children feel more comfortable when routines provide some consistency and predictability.

State the Positive

We often seem to more readily give our attention to those who misbehave. While we should not ignore misbehavior, we can frequently redirect it by simply pointing out the opposite—the positive. Try it and watch your children change their behavior. Find one or two doing the right action: use their names as you say what they are doing well and thank them. You'll be amazed how the other children look and copy the good behavior you have identified. Children know when they are acting up and change when they realize that it's the positive that gains the attention and approval they really desire. If your emphasis on the positive does not work, then pull individuals aside and quietly help them understand appropriate behavior.

Give Choices

Presenting choices helps children develop decision-making skills and helps them own the consequences of their decisions. Ask a child who is misbehaving if he or she needs help, or something else. The question may present enough of a decision to help redirect the behavior. Or you might ask if the child would like to join other children in one or more alternative activities. If children either can't decide or refuse, tell them you will count to three, then decide for them if necessary. Then you choose. Most of the time, children will make appropriate choices. Be sure to praise them for good choices.

Address Physical Aggression

Deal with physical aggression quickly and lovingly. Isolate aggressive children in a safe place in clear view of yourself and others. If you need a child to leave the room, be sure another teacher or responsible volunteer accompanies the child. Contact the parents of all the children involved in the altercation. Keep a record of the details of what happened.

Noah's Big Boat

BIBLE STORY:

Noah and the Ark
Genesis 6:1—9:17

BIBLE TRUTH:

I can trust God to keep his promises.

BIBLE VERSE:

He is always there to help us in times of trouble.
(Psalm 46:1b)

Some children unfortunately may have had experiences with people who acted in untrustworthy ways and broke a promise. Teach them that God is someone they can always trust and lean on; he will always keep his promises. No matter what storms blow into their lives, they can know God will always be with them.

⭐ In this lesson, children will **hear** the story of how God kept his promise to Noah by keeping him and his family safe in the ark.

⭐ In this lesson, children will **learn** that they can trust God to keep his promises.

⭐ In this lesson, children will **remember** that God promises to always be with us, especially in times of trouble.

Lesson One Snapshot

Get List:

- ☐ 1 copy of the *Hold'em-Up* reproducible (page 10) per child
- ☐ Scissors
- ☐ Crayons
- ☐ Large craft sticks
- ☐ Stapler
- ☐ Optional: Cotton balls, blue construction paper, glue sticks
- ☐ CD and CD player
- ☐ Colored streamers
- ☐ 4 beach towels
- ☐ Construction toys
- ☐ Blocks
- ☐ Empty boxes
- ☐ Stuffed animals
- ☐ Coffee filters
- ☐ Washable markers
- ☐ Eye dropper or straw
- ☐ Water
- ☐ Paper plate
- ☐ Butcher paper
- ☐ Tortilla chip scoops
- ☐ Canned cheese spread
- ☐ Pretzel sticks
- ☐ Bible
- ☐ Fruit ring cereal
- ☐ Small plastic bags
- ☐ 1 copy of *Home Connections* (page 15) for each child

The Heart of the Story:

Noah's experience shows us that God is trustworthy to keep his promises, even through rough stuff. Turbulent times come. We, and others, might even question where we place our trust.

During the hard and lonely times, grab on to the ray of hope that God gives you—his everlasting presence. Teach your little ones that they can trust God in difficult times. God promises to always be with us. We can trust him to keep us afloat.

Hold'em-Up
Bible Story Reproducible Page

- 1 copy of this page for each child
- Scissors
- Crayons
- Large craft sticks
- Stapler
- Optional: Cotton balls, blue construction paper, glue sticks

Copy and cut out the large rectangular figure for each child. Have the children color the pictures. You might have the children glue cotton to the clouds and blue paper for water beneath the ark. Fold in half on the dotted line so that both pictures show. Staple the top third of a craft stick between the sides for a handle. Staple the edges together.

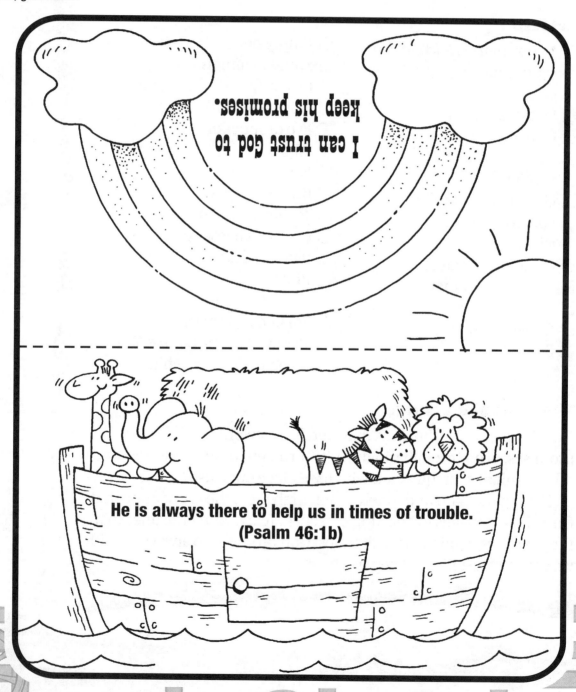

I can trust God to keep his promises.

He is always there to help us in times of trouble.
(Psalm 46:1b)

Round'em-Up

Use these *Round'em-Up* activities to gather the children or anytime you need a quick group activity for a transition or filler.

Bible Story Link

* CD and CD player
* Colored streamers

A Rainbow of Promises

Tell the children God keeps his promises. We remember he keeps his promises every time we see a rainbow. Tell the children they will have fun making colorful rainbows as they move to music. Hand out one or more two-foot pieces of colorful streamer to each child. When you play the music, have the children stand or move as they wave their streamers back and forth over their heads. When the music stops, the children freeze.

Game

* 4 beach towels

Safe in the Ark

Spread four towels on the floor with a good amount of space between each one. *Note: If you're not doing the activity on carpet, you may need to anchor the towels with tape or just outline rectangles on the floor with tape.* Have the children stand separately or as small groups on any or all of the towels. Tell them the towels are arks. As long as they are standing on an ark they are safe. Then tell them that when you call out, "Build the ark," the children must get off their towel arks and run to a different one, but try to not get tagged by you.

Song/Fingerplay

T-R-U-S-T

Sing the following lyrics to the tune of "B-I-N-G-O."

God is with you, you should know,
he's always there beside you.
T-R-U-S-T
T-R-U-S-T
T-R-U-S-T
Trust in God; he's always with you.

Show Me

Rock the Boat

Have the children show you how they can rock like a boat on their backs, stomachs, knees and bottoms. Then have the children find partners. Have them show you how they can rock like boats while holding hands. You can have them rock slowly or fast. You can have them show you a boat in a little storm and a boat in a big storm. Have fun rocking the boat. Talk about how God was with Noah even when the boat was rocking.

Bible Story

Hands-on Activities

These activities work well for large or small groups of children, or as stations, to introduce and/or reinforce the Bible story.

Noah's Big Boat

- Construction toys
- Blocks
- Empty boxes
- Stuffed animals

Tell the children that an ark is a very large boat. Provide construction toys, blocks and various boxes for the children to build big boats. Provide stuffed animals to fill the boats. Talk about how Noah built a big boat, that God used just as he promised, to keep Noah and the animals safe.

Raindrop Rainbows

- Coffee filters
- Washable markers
- Paper plate
- Eye dropper or straw
- Water

Hand out a coffee filter to each child. Have the children draw several curved lines an equal distance apart or some simple stick-figure pictures on their coffee filters using washable markers. Place the coffee filters over a paper plate to catch drips. Then use an eyedropper or the end of a straw to drop raindrops of water onto the filters. Watch the colors blend into a rainbow. Talk about how rainbows remind us that God kept his promises to Noah.

Bible Memory

He is always there to help us in times of trouble. (Psalm 46:1b)

- Butcher paper
- Scissors
- Marker

Before class, cut butcher paper into large cloud shapes, one per child. Tell the children that God was with Noah throughout the storm and especially whenever he might have felt he was in trouble. Ask the children to name their fears or what troubles them. Write their responses on the clouds. Then spread the clouds, long steps apart, on the floor in a circle. Have each child stand on a cloud. Have the children repeat the Bible Verse with you as they step from cloud to cloud for each word. Repeat several times.

Boat Bites

- Tortilla chip scoops
- Canned cheese spread
- Pretzel sticks

Before class, break the pretzel sticks into small pieces. These pieces will represent the animals in the ark. In class, give each child a few tortilla chip scoops filled with a little cheese. Have the children add pieces of pretzel sticks as if animals in the ark. Talk about how God kept Noah and the animals safe in the ark. We can trust God because he keeps his promises. *Note: Check with parents for any food allergies children may have.*

Bible Story Time

- Bible
- Completed *Hold'em-Up* for each child (from page 10)

Gather your children for Story Time; be sure all the children have their *Hold'em-Ups* ready to go. **As I tell the Bible story, I need you to listen for some special words. When you hear the word <u>boat</u>, show me your boat. When you hear the word <u>promise</u>, show me your rainbow.** Hold up a Bible for the children to see.

In the book of Genesis, there is a story about a man named Noah.

Noah was both kind and good. He always did just what he should.

He loved God with all his heart and trusted God right from the start.

But other people had turned evil and bad. This made God feel very sad.

So God asked Noah to build a <u>boat</u>. *(children hold up boat)* **"I'll send a flood, but you will float."**

God <u>promised</u> *(children hold up rainbow)* **Noah that he would keep Noah safe.**

So Noah built a great big <u>boat</u>. *(children hold up boat)*

Then one fine day the boat was done, but Noah's work had just begun.

God helped Noah start a zoo. The creatures came on the <u>boat</u> *(children hold up boat)* **two by two.**

Then Noah and his family got on board. God shut the door and thunder roared.

It rained for 40 days and nights; everyone was full of fright.

But God kept them all safe and sound. He kept his <u>promise</u> *(children hold up rainbow)* **as they found. Then colors flashed across the sky. God made a rainbow–my, oh my!**

God made this <u>promise</u> *(children hold up rainbow)* **to his friend. "I'll never send a flood again."**

God's <u>promises</u> *(children hold up rainbow)* **are always true–true for Noah, true for you.**

And God is always with you, too!

- **Who told Noah to build a boat?** *(God)*
- **Who kept his promise to Noah?** *(God)*
- **Who can you trust to keep a promise?** *(God)*

Send'em-Off

- Fruit ring cereal
- Small plastic bags
- Completed *Hold'em-Ups*

Prayer

Talk about how God took care of Noah. Then ask the children about times God has taken care of them. Then have the children repeat this prayer after you: **Dear God, thank you for taking care of us and being with us. Thank you for keeping your promises. We love and trust you. In Jesus' name, amen.**

Cleanup

Have the children pretend to be the animals on the ark. As they clean up, they must have a partner, two-by-two. After a minute of clean-up time, have them find a different partner and become a different animal. Repeat.

Homeward Bound

As the children leave, make sure they have their completed *Hold'em-Ups* they made for Bible Story Time. Also, as they leave, give them some fruit ring cereal in a small baggie. Tell them the colors in the cereal can remind them of the colors of the rainbow. God keeps his promises just as he did for Noah. *Note: Check with parents for any food allergies children may have.*

- **What does the rainbow remind you of?**
- **Who keeps his promises?**
- **Who can you trust?**

Home Connections

It's a Snap!

Title: Noah's Big Boat

Bible Story:
Noah and the Ark
Genesis 6:1—9:17

Bible Truth: I can trust God to keep his promises.

Bible Verse: He is always there to help us in times of trouble. (Psalm 46:1b)

- In this lesson, your child **heard** the story of how God kept his promise to Noah by keeping him and his family safe in the ark.

- In this lesson, your child **learned** that he or she can trust God to keep his promises.

- In this lesson, your child **remembered** that God promises to always be with us, especially in times of trouble.

We trust people, and that's a good thing. But sometimes, people let us down by not keeping their promises. However, God always keeps his promises. Help your child understand and remember this truth, and that God is always with us, even during the stormy times of our lives.

Home Connections

These are items that were used during the Bible story lesson that might be commonly found in your home. When your child sees, plays with or uses one of the items listed, help him or her connect it with the Bible story.

Rainbows: God used a rainbow as a sign of his promise to Noah. A rainbow can help us remember that God always keeps his promises. Use this concept when using the colors of the rainbow too. The order of the colors of the rainbow is red, orange, yellow, green, blue, indigo and violet.

Fruit ring cereal: The colors remind us of the colors in a rainbow.

Boats: Anytime you see a boat, remind your child about the special boat Noah built that was called an ark. Encourage your child with these words, "God took care of Noah when he was in his great big boat. God will take care of you too."

Tortilla chips: Tortilla chips shaped like scoops served as little boats during this lesson. Anytime you bite into these chips can be an opportunity to talk about this Bible lesson and the story of Noah in the ark.

Keeping Connected

Here's a fun and easy song used in class to reinforce the Bible lesson about Noah. Have fun singing with your child to remember the Bible story lesson.

T-R-U-S-T *(Song/Finger Play)*
Sing to the tune of "B-I-N-G-O"

> *God is with you, you should know,*
> *he's always there beside you.*
> *T-R-U-S-T*
> *T-R-U-S-T*
> *T-R-U-S-T*
> *Trust in God he's with you.*

Prayer

Talk about how God took care of Noah and then share an experience of your own. Ask your child and other family members about times God has taken care of them. Then pray together: **Dear God, thank you for taking care of us and being with us. Thank you for keeping your promises. We love and trust you. In Jesus' name, amen.**

The Teeny Tiny Basket Boat

BIBLE STORY:

Baby Moses
Exodus 2:1–10

BIBLE TRUTH:

I am precious
to God!

BIBLE VERSE:

Trust in the LORD
with all your heart.
(Proverbs 3:5a)

Every child is precious to God because he made each one. Teach your young children that they can trust God at all times. He will always take care of them, and he has special plans for their lives.

★ In this lesson, children will **hear** the story of baby Moses as he traveled down the Nile in his teeny tiny basket boat.

★ In this lesson, children will **learn** they are precious to God.

★ In this lesson, children will **remember** they can trust God.

Lesson Two Snapshot

Get List:

☐ 1 copy of the *Hold'em-Up* reproducible (page 18) per child
☐ Scissors
☐ Tape
☐ Crayons and markers
☐ Tub of water
☐ Items to sink or float
☐ Large blue beach towel
☐ Optional: Blue painter's tape
☐ Paper baking cups

☐ Large paper cups
☐ 2 or more large laundry baskets
☐ Bible
☐ Bananas
☐ Plastic knives
☐ Bear-shaped graham crackers
☐ Paper plates
☐ Baskets (1 per child or pair of children)
☐ 1 copy of *Home Connections* (page 23) for each child

The Heart of the Story:

Moses went through some turbulent waters in his lifetime on the Nile, as an infant, and at the Red Sea later in life. This lesson navigates his first experience, escaping what seemed like certain death. Moses' mother and sister knew that everyone is precious to God. That helped them trust God to take care of baby Moses, even as they planned, prepared and then pushed Moses onto the river in his basket boat.

Each of us are just as precious to God as Moses. Knowing this at whatever age we are helps us trust God, especially when the waters of life around us seem rough, scary or uncertain.

Hold'em-Up

Bible Story Reproducible Page

* 1 copy of the reproducibles on this page for each child
* Scissors
* Tape
* Crayons and markers

Copy and cut out Figures 1 and 2 for each child. Have the children color baby Moses and the basket boat. Fold the baby Moses figure in half to make a stick. Tape the two bottom pieces together. Fold the basket figure and cut a slit on the fold where indicated by the solid line. Show the children how to place the stick ends through the slit in the basket boat. Show them how to move the stick to pop Moses out of the basket.

Figure 1

Figure 2

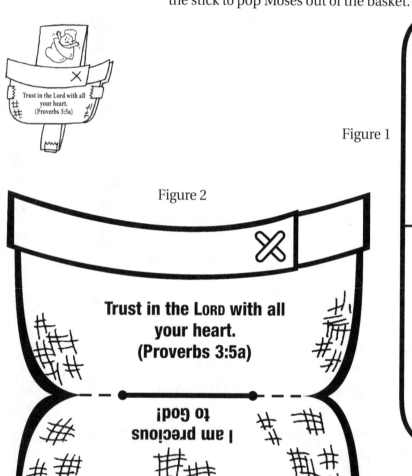

**Trust in the LORD with all your heart.
(Proverbs 3:5a)**

I am precious to God!

Round'em-Up

Use these *Round'em-Up* activites to gather the children or anytime you need a quick and easy group activity for transition or a filler.

Bible Story Link

* Tub of water
* Items to sink or float

Sink or Float?

Will it sink or will it float? Gather different objects. Show each item to the children. Have the children predict whether the object will sink or float. Then place the object in a tub of water. At the end of the activity, talk about how boats float on water. Link this to how the Bible story will be about a baby who floats down a river in a teeny tiny basket boat.

Game

* Large blue beach towel
* Optional: Blue painter's tape

Jumping the River

Spread a large blue towel on the floor, then scrunch in the long sides as if making some ripples on a river. Have the children line up and jump over the river. After each child has a turn, extend the sides of the towel out farther, so the river is a little wider. Everyone takes turns jumping again. Continue playing until the towel is fully extended. *Note: If your floor is slick and the towel might slide, substitute the alternative painter's tape. Just peel it up and move it to make the river wider.*

Song/ Fingerplay

God Cares for Moses and Me

Look up and down the river.
(hand to brow, looking)
To see what we can see.
A little tiny baby,
(pretend to rock a baby)
As happy as can be.
God cared for baby Moses
(pretend to rock a baby)
And God will care for me!
(point to self)

Show Me

* Paper baking cups

Balancing Boats

Hand each child a paper baking cup. Tell the children this is their little boat. Have them show how they can keep their cup on an elbow, on a shoulder or on their heads. Then have them repeat each of these positions, plus a knee, while standing on one foot. Increase the challenge having them do all with their eyes closed. Talk about how boats float.

Bible Story
Hands-on Activities

These activities work well for large or small groups of children, or as stations, to introduce and/or reinforce the Bible story.

Activity 1

Blow a Boat

Cut the tops down on paper cups so that only an inch or two remains. Label or decorate the cups to distinguish each one. Have the children set the cups on tabletops. Challenge them to blow their boats to the opposite side of the table.

* Large paper cups
* Scissors
* Crayons or markers

Activity 2

Basket Boats

Line up laundry basket "boats." Have the children take turns pushing them, or you can be the designated pusher as they boat "downstream" in the laundry baskets. Be sure to steer clear of rocks, sticks and other river hazards. As children wait their turn, they can pretend to be frogs hopping along the shore of the Nile River.

* 2 or more large laundry baskets

Activity 3

Bible Memory

Trust in the LORD with all your heart. (Proverbs 3:5a)

* Bible

Show the children Proverbs 3:5 in your Bible. Tell them this verse teaches us to trust God. We can trust him because we are precious to God. You might wish to call out each child's name before singing each round of this Bible Verse song.

(Song/Finger Play) **Trust in the Lord**
Sing to the tune of "Wheels on the Bus Go 'Round and 'Round."

Trust in the Lord with all your heart,
all your heart, all your heart.
Trust in the Lord with all your heart,
all day long.

Activity 4

Banana Boats

Cut the bananas in half lengthwise to make little boats. Pass a dish of bear-shaped graham crackers to use as baby Moses. Have the children place baby Moses in the banana boat. *Note: Check with parents for any food allergies children may have.*

Have the children sing to the tune of "Row, Row, Row Your Boat."
Float, float, float your boat gently down the Nile,
Merrily, merrily, merrily, merrily, give a great big smile.

* Bananas
* Plastic knives
* Bear-shaped graham crackers
* Paper plates

Bible Story Time

- Bible
- A completed *Hold'em-Up* made from the reproducible on page 18 for each child

Gather your children for Story Time; be sure all the children have their *Hold'em-Ups* ready to go. Hold up a Bible for the children to see. **Moses was a great man in the Old Testament of the Bible. But before he became a great man, he was little bitty baby … just like all of you were babies once. Everyone pop up your babies.** Have the children pop up baby Moses out of their *Hold'em-Ups.* **This is baby Moses. Every time you hear me say the name <u>Moses</u>, show me baby Moses.**

The Bible tells us that when <u>Moses</u> was born, his mother loved him very much. But she was afraid for her baby boy <u>Moses</u>. There was a very mean and bad king who wanted all the baby boys to be killed, even baby <u>Moses</u>.

<u>Moses</u>' mother thought and thought of a way to protect her son. She made a teeny, tiny, basket boat and put little baby <u>Moses</u> inside. Then she took the teeny, tiny, basket boat with <u>Moses</u> inside and put it in the mighty Nile River. She trusted God to take care of baby <u>Moses</u>.

<u>Moses</u> floated in his teeny, tiny, basket boat down the river. The river was rough and scary. <u>Moses</u> could have fallen out of his basket or bumped his head on a rock. He could have even been eaten by a crocodile! But God took care of <u>Moses</u> and kept him safe. <u>Moses</u> floated in his basket boat right past the mean soldiers. Eventually <u>Moses</u> was scooped out of the river by a very special lady, and he was saved.

<u>Moses</u> was very precious to God, and God took care of <u>Moses</u>. You are precious to God too. You can trust God to take care of you, too, just like he took care of <u>Moses</u>.

- **Why was Moses floating in a basket boat?** *(his mother put him there)*
- **Who is precious to God?** *(Moses, you, me, all of us, everyone)*
- **Who can you trust to take care of you?** *(God, family members, friends, teachers)*

Send'em-Off

* Baskets (1 for each child or pair of children)
* Completed *Hold'em-Up* for each child

Teacher Tip

Sometimes you may have a child who does not want to join in any of the activities. Tell him, "We would love for you to join us whenever you are ready." After a few minutes, ask him if he would be willing to help you. He could color something for you or simply hold something for you. Some children need time to watch what is going on before engaging in play. Some children need a little extra TLC and encouragement.

Itty Bitty Bible Facts

In Bible times, people did not have bathtubs. They would go take their baths in a river. What do you think that would be like?

Prayer

Explain that prayer is simply talking with God. Have the children repeat this prayer after you: **Dear God, thank you for our precious friend, _____ (name of a child in the class). We trust you to take care of _____ (same name) today and tomorrow. In Jesus' name, amen.**

Cleanup

Give the children different sized and shaped baskets. Tell them these are their basket clean-up boats. When they pick up an item, have them place it in the basket. Then have the child find someone to hand the basket to. Have the children continue to pick up items and pass the baskets around. As they hand over a basket, they can repeat the phrase, "You are precious to God; trust in him."

Homeward Bound

As the children leave, make sure they have their completed *Hold'em-Ups* they made for Bible Story Time. Have the children sing or say this simple rhyme as they leave.

> *Rock-a-bye Moses in your wee boat,*
> *that your momma made to keep you afloat.*
> *God will take care of you as you glide,*
> *in and around the riverside.*

* **What does your boat remind you of?**
* **Tell me your favorite part of today's lesson.**
* **Who loves you and thinks you are very precious?**

Home Connections

It's a Snap!

Title: The Teeny Tiny Basket Boat

Bible Story: Baby Moses
Exodus 2:1–10

Bible Truth: I am precious to God!

Bible Verse: Trust in the LORD with all your heart. (Proverbs 3:5a)

- In this lesson, your child **heard** the story of baby Moses as he traveled down the Nile in his teeny tiny basket boat.

- In this lesson, your child **learned** he or she is precious to God.

- In this lesson, your child **remembered** he or she can trust God.

aby Moses could have had all kinds of troubles as he floated down the mighty Nile River in a teeny tiny basket boat. He could have tipped over into the river or bumped his head on a rock. But God had different plans for Moses. God took care of Moses and kept him safe. Your child is sure to experience many bumps and bruises in life. Help your child understand that God loves him or her deeply. Your child is very precious to God. Your child can trust God because God highly values your child.

Home Connections

These are items that were used during the Bible story lesson that might be commonly found in your home. When your child sees or plays with one of the items mentioned below, help make the connection to the Bible story.

Laundry basket: These were used as little basket boats floating down the Nile River. As you push or pull your child in a laundry-basket boat, remind your child how God was with Moses when he was floating in a basket boat.

Blue towel: A blue towel (or maybe blue painter's tape) made a pretend river on the floor during class. Do the same and have your child jump over your towel river. Remind your child how God was with baby Moses as he floated down the Nile River in a basket boat.

Paper cups: The tops of paper cups were cut down to make little boats. The boats could then be used on a tabletop or in the bathtub. As your child plays with the cup, remind him or her of how God was with Moses in his little boat.

Keeping Connected

Here are two simple activities that were used in class during the Bible story lesson of The Teeny Tiny Basket Boat. Use these activities to help your child remember the Bible story lesson.

Sink or Float?
Will it sink or will it float? Gather different objects. Show each item to your child. Have him or her predict whether the object will sink or float. Then place the object in a tub of water. At the end of the activity, talk about how boats float on water. Link this to the Bible story of baby Moses floating down a river in a teeny tiny basket boat.

Trust in the Lord *(Song/Finger Play)*
Sing to the tune of "Wheels on the Bus Go 'Round and 'Round."

Trust in the Lord with all your heart, all your heart, all your heart.
Trust in the Lord with all your heart, all day long.

God's Ten Special Rules

BIBLE STORY:

The Ten
Commandments
Exodus 19—20

BIBLE TRUTH:

God wants me
to do what is right.

BIBLE VERSE:

I will obey
your word.
(Psalm 119:17b)

To obey does not mean just sit and stay. To obey does not always mean to do what you are told. Obeying God is doing what is right. We obey God not because we have to, but because we want to. Help the children understand that these are God's 10 rules. When you obey God's rules, your heart will be filled with eternal riches.

* In this lesson, children will **hear** that God gave us 10 very special rules that are found in the Bible.

* In this lesson, children will **learn** that God wants us to do what is right.

* In this lesson, children will **remember** to obey God's Word.

Lesson Three Snapshot

Get List:

- ☐ 1 copy of the *Hold'em-Up* reproducible (page 26) per child
- ☐ Scissors
- ☐ Tape
- ☐ Crayons and markers
- ☐ Masking tape
- ☐ Beanbags or sponges
- ☐ Optional: Sets of 10 pennies or blocks
- ☐ Small foil pans
- ☐ Sand
- ☐ Empty egg cartons
- ☐ Small stones that fit into egg carton holders
- ☐ Bible
- ☐ Sticky note
- ☐ Paper plates
- ☐ Craft sticks
- ☐ Canned frosting
- ☐ Chocolate chips or small candies
- ☐ Graham crackers
- ☐ 1 copy of *Home Connections* (page 31) for each child

The Heart of the Story:

God created us to want to do what is right and gave us the freedom and ability to make the choice. But obedience is not automatic. We must continually make that choice whether we are five, 55 or 105.

Learning what is right and how to do it is often easier when we are young. But that is no excuse when we are older! Of course, knowing our creator's rules and directions for our lives is a great help. Learning that God has those rules for us and where we can find them is important.

This lesson helps lay a strong foundation for you and the children in your class to obey God. Help the children you teach to set that foundation and build on it for a happy, healthy and God-honoring life. God loves us and wants the best for us. He gave us 10 incredibly special rules that can show us how to have a wonderful life!

Hold'em-Up
Bible Story Reproducible Page

* 1 copy of the reproducible on this page for each child
* Scissors
* Tape
* Crayons or markers

Copy and cut out all of the figures for each child. Have the children color the two stone tablets. Use tape to attach the strips to form a loop on the center-back of the tablets. Show the children how to slip a hand in each loop on the backs to hold up the tablets. Raise the 5 first and the 10 second.

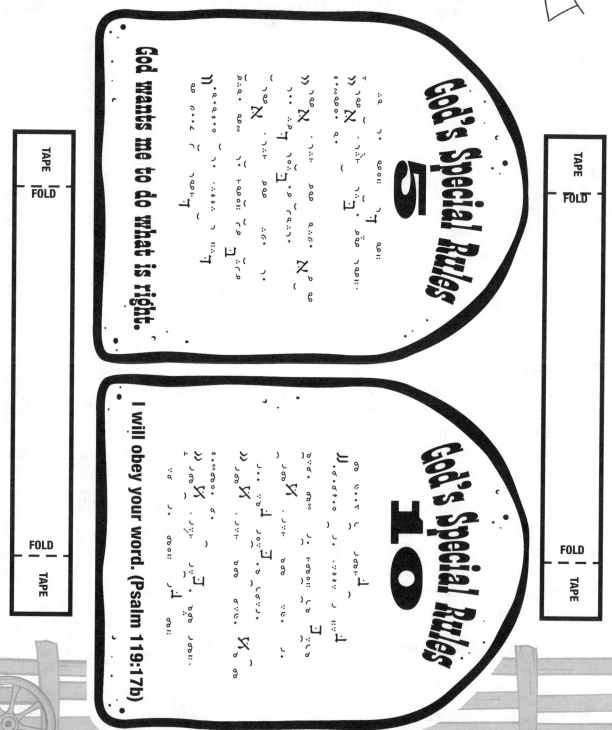

TAPE
FOLD

God's Special Rules 5

God wants me to do what is right.

FOLD
TAPE

TAPE
FOLD

God's Special Rules 10

I will obey your word. (Psalm 119:17b)

FOLD
TAPE

Round'em-Up

Use these *Round'em-Up* activities to gather the children or anytime you need a quick group activity for a transition or filler.

God's Ten Rules

* Masking tape
* Beanbags or sponges

Before class, mark a large circle on the floor with masking tape. Then use masking tape to place 10 large Xs on the floor inside the circle. Be sure to scatter the Xs.

In class, have the children stand outside the circle and count the Xs. Talk about how God has 10 very special rules for us to follow. Then challenge the children to toss beanbags or sponges onto the Xs. They can run in to get a beanbag that misses an X, but must toss from the outside of the circle. Leave the beanbags that land on an X. Try to cover each X. When all the beanbags are on Xs, have everyone shout, "God's 10 special rules!"

Obey Rules
(played like Simon Says)

God gave us rules to obey to help us do what is right. This Obey Rules game reinforces this.

Tell the children to stand and follow every instruction you give if you first say, "Obey rules." Any instruction given without you first saying, "Obey rules," should not be followed. Those doing actions they shouldn't sit down for one turn.

Directions might be: rub your tummy, pat your head, stand on one foot, hop on one foot and so on. Talk about how God wants us to obey his 10 special rules.

Rules to Follow God

Sing the following lyrics to the tune of "Ten Little Indians." As the children sing, have them hold up the corresponding number of fingers.

One little, two little, three little rules.
Four little, five little, six little rules.
Seven little, eight little, nine little rules,
ten rules to follow God.

The Number Ten

* Optional: Sets of 10 pennies or blocks

Have the children show you 10 fingers or for more challenge, make their fingers resemble the numerals in 10. Then encourage them to show you the number 10 in a different way. They might use a finger to draw the number 10 in the air. Or they might use one finger on one hand for the one, and a fist on the second hand for the zero. See how many ways they can come up with the number 10, the number of God's special rules. For younger children, you might provide several objects, such as pennies or blocks, in groups of 10 for them to count.

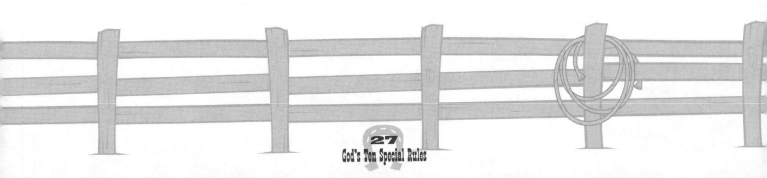

Bible Story
Hands-on Activities

These activities work well for large or small groups of children, or as stations, to introduce and/or reinforce the Bible story.

Writing on the Stone

- ☀ Small foil pans
- ☀ Sand

Put a little sand in small foil pans. Have the children use their fingers to draw pictures in the sand. Let the children write the numbers 1 through 10 in the sand. Talk about how the sand resembles stone. Talk about how God used his finger to etch his 10 rules onto stone tablets. God gave us 10 great rules because he loves us very much.

God's Ten Rockin' Rules

- ☀ Empty egg cartons
- ☀ Scissors
- ☀ Little rocks that fit into egg carton holders
- ☀ Marker

Cut egg cartons so they have only 10 egg holders. Provide 10 small rocks for each carton you prepare. Tell the children God gave us 10 great rockin' rules. Have the children put a rock into each egg holder. As they empty and fill the carton, have them shout, "God's 10 Rockin' Rules!" You might number each egg holder, 1-10.

Bible Memory

I will obey your word.
(Psalm 119:17b)

- ☀ Bible
- ☀ Sticky note

Hold up the Bible for the children to see. **This is a Bible. The Bible has God's Word written for us.** Point out Psalm 119:17 to each child and place a sticky note nearby for easy reference. **The Bible says, "I will obey your word." God wants us to obey the words in the Bible. This includes his 10 special rules.** Have the children sit in a circle. Pass the Bible around the circle. At each pass, everyone say together one word of the Bible verse.

Tasty Tablets

- ☀ Paper plates
- ☀ Craft sticks
- ☀ Canned frosting
- ☀ Chocolate chips or small candies
- ☀ Graham crackers

Hand out two graham crackers to each child. Tell them God wrote his 10 special rules on two stone tablets. Have them pretend the crackers are their stone tablets. Use the craft sticks to spread some frosting on the tablets. Then have them add 10 items, five to each tablet, such as chocolate chips or small candy pieces. Talk about how God's 10 rules help us to do what is right. *Note: Check with parents for any food allergies children may have.*

Bible Story Time

- Bible
- A completed *Hold'em-Up* made from the reproducible page for each child

Gather your children for Story Time; be sure all the children have their *Hold'em-Ups* ready to go. **Every time you hear the words "10 special rules," you say, "Five and 10 special rules to obey. Five and 10 special rules, hip-hip-hooray!"** When the children say five, have them hold up one hand (tablet), then the other hand (tablet) when they say 10. Have them hold up both hands for "hip-hip-hooray!" Have the children practice the phrase and the hand motions. Hold up a Bible for the children to see.

This is my Bible. The Bible is God's Word written for everyone to read or listen to and memorize so they learn about God and his love for us. God has given us every word that is in the Bible.

Some of the words in the Bible are God's <u>10 special rules</u>. God gave these to Moses to give to us. Here is how it happened.

God covered a mountain with a big cloud. People couldn't see the mountain since it was covered. The people could see lightning and hear thunder and a loud trumpet blast. God came to the mountain in the cloud and the mountain shook like an earthquake and the trumpet became even louder. The people knew God was on the mountain but they couldn't see him. Moses climbed up the mountain to meet God.

There, on top of the mountain, surrounded by a cloud, God gave Moses the <u>10 special rules</u> God wanted all people to have. Moses listened to get these rules because they help us know about God and how we can do what is right.

God told Moses all <u>10 special rules</u>. Moses listened very carefully so he could follow the rules and also tell others the rules. But God also wrote his <u>10 special rules</u> on two stone tablets so they would last a long time. God didn't use a pencil or a pen to write. He carved the words of the rules into the stone with his finger!

We call these rules the Ten Commandments. God gave us the Ten Commandments because he loves us very much and wants to help us do what is right. We can be glad and thank God for his <u>10 special rules</u>.

- **How many rules did God give us?** *(10)*
- **Why did God give us 10 rules to follow?** *(because he wants us to do what is right)*
- **Who should obey God's 10 rules?** *(we should, everyone should)*

Send'em-Off

- ⭐ 2 small stones
- ⭐ Completed *Hold'em-Up* for each child

Teacher Tip

Be sure the stones you use for today's activities are larger than 2 inches in diameter to assure your stones do not present a choking hazard. Error toward too big rather than too small. You can always substitute small marshmallows for these activities.

Itty Bitty Bible Facts

God gave Moses the Ten Commandments in Exodus 20. But the Bible doesn't mention the stone tablets until Exodus 32:15. God then explains he wrote on the tablets himself.

Prayer

Have the children sit in a circle. Tell them you are going to pass two small stones. Talk about how the two small stones remind you of the two stone tablets mentioned in the Bible story. Have the children thank God for his 10 special rules. Place the two small stones in the first child's hand. Have that child say, "Dear God, thank you for your 10 special rules. In Jesus' name, amen." Then pass the stones to the next child, who repeats the prayer. Continue around the circle.

Cleanup

Challenge the children to pick up 10 items as they clean. Have them show you their 10 items. Ask the children what the number 10 means to them. Then tell them it reminds you of the 10 special rules God wants us to follow.

Homeward Bound

As the children leave, make sure they have their completed *Hold'em-Ups* they made for Bible Story Time. Have the children count to the number 10 using their fingers, if they wish, as they leave.

- ⭐ **How many special rules does God have?**
- ⭐ **Who should follow God's special rules?**

Home Connections

It's a Snap!

Title: God's Ten Special Rules

Bible Story: The Ten Commandments *Exodus 19—20*

Bible Truth: God wants me to do what is right.

Bible Verse: I will obey your word. (Psalm 119:17b)

- In this lesson, your child **heard** that God gave us 10 very special rules that are found in the Bible.

- In this lesson, your child **learned** that God wants us to do what is right.

- In this lesson, your child **remembered** to obey God's Word.

What feeling words come to you when you hear the word "obey"? Most people connect the word "obey" to a negative list of "don'ts, shouldn'ts and better nots." Obeying God is about us wanting to do what is right, not obeying because you have to or to avoid punishment. God gave us the Ten Commandments out of love, protection and guidance. These rules tell us what is important to him. Following God's rules are about doing what you know will please the one who loves you the most and who created you. Teach your child to "obey" God's Word.

Home Connections

These items that were used during the Bible story lesson might be commonly found in your home. When your child sees or plays with one of the items mentioned below, help make the connection to the Bible story.

Stones or Rocks: These were used throughout the Bible story lesson as reminders of the tablets on which God wrote the Ten Commandants. You might wish to go for a walk and pick up some rocks. Talk about how God's 10 special rules were written on stone tablets.

The Number 10: The number 10 was used throughout the entire lesson as a reminder of how many special rules God has for us. As your child counts out 10 objects or simply counts to 10, talk about how the number 10 reminds you of God's special rules.

Keeping Connected

Here are two simple activities that were used in the Bible story lesson of God's 10 special rules. Use these activities to help your child remember the Bible story lesson.

Rules to Follow God (*Song/Finger Play*)
Sing to the tune of "Ten Little Indians" and hold up the corresponding number of fingers.

> *One little, two little, three little rules.*
> *Four little, five little, six little rules.*
> *Seven little, eight little, nine little rules,*
> *ten rules to follow God.*

God's 10 Rockin' Rules
Cut egg cartons so there are only 10 egg holders and number each one. Find 10 small rocks. Tell your child how God gave us 10 great rockin' rules. Have your child put a rock into each egg holder and count 1-10. When the carton is full, shout, "God's 10 Rockin' Rules!"

Tabernacle Togetherness

BIBLE STORY:

Building the Tabernacle
Exodus 25—26;
Numbers 7

BIBLE TRUTH:

God wants us to
work together.

BIBLE VERSE:

Don't forget to
share with others.
(Hebrews 13:16a)

I t's mine … give it to me … I'll do it! These words flow easily from the mouths of children ages three to five. And believe it or not, developmentally they are designed this way. Give your little ones many opportunities for growth as you encourage them to share and cooperate with others.

☆ In this lesson, children will **hear** the story of how God's people helped each other build God's tabernacle.

☆ In this lesson, children will **learn** that God wants us to work together.

☆ In this lesson, children will **remember** to serve one another in love as they work together.

Lesson Four Snapshot

Get List:

- [ ] 1 copy of *Hold'em-Up* reproducible (page 34) per child
- [ ] Scissors
- [ ] Tape
- [ ] Crayons or markers
- [ ] Blocks
- [ ] Paper towels
- [ ] 10–15 balloons
- [ ] One small tarp or old shower curtain
- [ ] Paper cups
- [ ] Tarp, sheets, blankets
- [ ] Tables or chairs
- [ ] Shoe box
- [ ] Various decorative items
- [ ] Glue stick
- [ ] Wrapping paper
- [ ] Various trail mix ingredients
- [ ] Bowls and spoons
- [ ] Bible
- [ ] Bowl of round, colorful cereal
- [ ] Large empty box or laundry basket
- [ ] 1″ squares of paper for each child
- [ ] 1 copy of *Home Connections* (page 39) for each child

The Heart of the Story:

God's people worked incredibly hard to build the tabernacle. In fact, it was pretty miraculous when you think about it. Everyone contributed something to help build God's house. It would have taken years to build without everyone's cooperation.

One lesson woven within this biblical account is that we can do so much more when we work together, share and cooperate for one common purpose. When it comes to God's work, we should set our eyes on him for direction and unity, especially if we have differences. Ask God to show you what he wants you to do with others to further his kingdom.

Hold'em-Up

Bible Story Reproducible Page

* 1 copy of the reproducible on this page for each child
* Scissors
* Tape
* Crayons or markers

Copy and then cut out both figures for each child. Have the children color the pictures. To make the tabernacle stand, cut on the solid line and fold on the dotted line. Place tab A over tab B and tape. To make the treasure box, cut on the solid lines and fold up on the dotted lines. Tape the tabs to the back of the sides. Then tape the box to tab A where indicated.

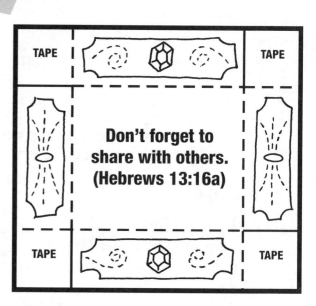

Don't forget to share with others. (Hebrews 13:16a)

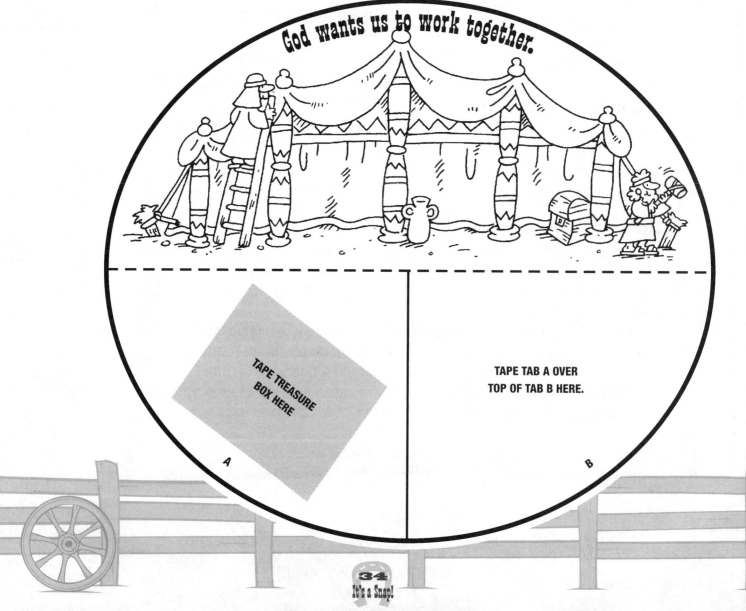

God wants us to work together.

TAPE TREASURE BOX HERE

A

TAPE TAB A OVER TOP OF TAB B HERE.

B

Round'em-Up

Use these *Round'em-Up* activities to gather the children or anytime you need a quick group activity for a transition or filler.

Bible Story Link

- Blocks
- Paper towel

Let's Build a Tabernacle

Have the children sit in a circle with the blocks spread among them. Talk about how everyone was needed to help build the tabernacle, which was a big tent for worshipping God. Have the children pass the blocks around the circle and then to you in the center of the circle. Use the blocks to build the walls of the tabernacle. Then use a paper towel draped over the top as the tent-like roof. As the children pass the blocks, have them repeat, **"Let's build a tabernacle, everyone help out. Share our things and share the work, then let's all scream and shout."**

Game

- 10–15 balloons
- One small tarp or old shower curtain

Bring the Gifts

Before class, blow up and tie the balloons. Spread the tarp on the floor. Disperse the balloons around the room. Tell the children the people worked together to bring gifts to the tabernacle. When you shout, "Bring the gifts!" the children work together to pick up the balloons and put them on the tarp. They cannot use their hands to carry the balloons. You can suggest alternatives such as using their knees or elbows. Once all the balloons are on the tarp, have the children pick up the edges and work together tossing the gifts (balloons) in the air, trying to keep all the gifts landing on the tarp, not the floor.

Song/Fingerplay

Cooperate!

Sing to the tune of "Jesus Loves Me."

Moms and dads and good friends too,
can help me when there's work to do.
I help, they help, it's just great!
God helps us co-op-er-ate.

Show Me

- Paper towels

Tent Tops

Hand each child a section of paper towel. Tell the children this is their tent top. Have the children try to make tents by blowing under the paper towels. How long can they keep one up in the air? Talk about how people in Bible times gathered at the tabernacle tent to worship God.

Bible Story
Hands-on Activities

These activities work well for large or small groups of children, or as stations, to introduce and/or reinforce the Bible story.

Build a Tabernacle

* Paper cups

Provide paper cups for building. Talk about how the people worked together to build a tabernacle for God. Have the children work together to see how high they can build their tabernacle. They might build a pyramid starting with a row of 10 cups, then add an additional row of nine cups, then eight cups and so on.

Tent Tabernacle

* Tarp, sheets, blankets
* Tables or chairs

Use a large tarp, sheet or blanket, and tables or chairs. Have the children work together to build a tabernacle. Then have the children find treasures such as pencils, papers, finished crafts, etc., around the room to bring to the tabernacle. Point out those children who are demonstrating cooperation by serving and helping each other.

Bible Memory

Don't forget to share with others. (Hebrews 13:16a)

* Shoe box
* Various decorative items
* Scissors
* Glue stick
* Wrapping paper

Use a shoe box, paper and other items to make a treasure box. As you make the treasure box, talk about how the people worked together, sharing with each other and bringing treasures for the tabernacle. When the box is finished, have the children sit in a circle. Pass the treasure box around the circle. As the box is handed from one child to the next, have everyone say, "Don't forget to share with others."

Tabernacle Trail Mix

* Various trail mix ingredients
* Paper cups
* Bowls and spoons

Get a few different items for the trail mix and put them into bowls. You might wish to use various items to represent different things in the real tabernacle: banana chips for gold, dried cranberries for scarlet yarn, pretzels for acacia wood, cinnamon hearts for spices and raisins for onyx stones. Have the children share and work together as they pass the items and take one scoop full of each to fill their cups. *Note: Check with parents for any food allergies children may have.*

Bible Story Time

* Bible
* A completed *Hold'em-Up* for each child (see page 34)
* Bowl of round, colorful cereal

Gather your children for Story Time; be sure all children have their *Hold'em-Ups* ready to go. Hold up a Bible for the children to see. **In the Bible, there is an amazing story about how God's people worked together to build a tabernacle for God. Then they shared with each other as they brought gifts for God to the tabernacle. As I tell the story, you are going to fill your tabernacle with gifts too.** After each phrase is read, have the children pass the bowl of "treasures" (colorful cereal) and take a piece to add to their tabernacles. *Note: Check with parents for any food allergies children may have.*

Let's build a tabernacle, we're gonna worship there.
Every house and family needs to do its share. *(children pass the treasures)*

Let's build a tabernacle.
We need lots of stuff, like scarlet yarn and onyx stones,
I hope we'll have enough. *(children pass the treasures)*

Let's build a tabernacle, we'll follow God's command.
Then God will come and guide us, as we travel through the land. *(children pass the treasures)*

Let's build a tabernacle, it's looking pretty nice.
All we need to finish up are incense, gems and spice. *(children pass the treasures)*

Let's build a tabernacle, our gifts we gladly bring.
We lay them at the altar as we worship God our King. *(children pass the treasures)*

We all built a tabernacle, everyone helped out.
We shared our things and shared the work,
so let's all scream and shout.

* **Who built the tabernacle?** *(the people)*
* **Who brought treasures to the tabernacle?** *(the people)*
* **Why did the people build the tabernacle?** *(to have a place to worship God)*

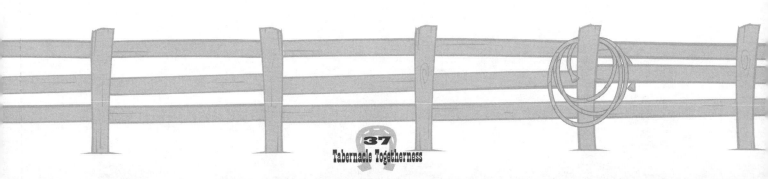

Send'em-Off

- Large empty box or laundry basket
- 1″ squares of paper for each child
- Completed *Hold'em-Up* for each child

Prayer

Have the children stand in a circle and join hands. Say this prayer aloud together: **Dear God, thank you for your circle of friends. Help us to be kind to each other. Help us to work together. In Jesus' name, amen.**

Then have the children, keeping their hands together, bunch into the circle as tightly as they can. Have them raise their hands in the air to form the top of a tabernacle. Then have them drop back to form their circle again. Point out children who are cooperating and working together.

Cleanup

Provide a large box or laundry basket for pairs of children to collect classroom supplies. Tell them they may only put in the items that they bring to you with a partner. Go around the room and shout out, "Bring treasures, treasures, treasures for our King!" As they bring their treasure with a partner say, "Thank you for working together." If they come by themselves, simply ask them to find a friend to share in the work. Affirm how quickly and easily the cleanup goes when we work together.

Homeward Bound

As the children leave, make sure they have their completed *Hold'em-Ups* they made for Bible Story Time. Take a one-inch square piece of paper and fold it in half making a tent top. Place a tent top in the children's hands. Tell them this tent top reminds us of how the people worked together to build God's tabernacle.

- **What do you remember when you see your tent top?**
- **What is one thing you can share with others?**

Home Connections

It's a Snap!

Title: Tabernacle Togetherness

Bible Story: Building the Tabernacle *Exodus 25—26; Numbers 7*

Bible Truth: God wants us to work together.

Bible Verse: Don't forget to share with others. (Hebrews 13:16a)

- In this lesson, your child **heard** the story of how God's people helped each other build God's tabernacle.

- In this lesson, your child **learned** that God wants us to work together.

- In this lesson, your child **remembered** to serve one another in love as they work together.

God's people accomplished an amazing feat—building the tabernacle by sharing and working together. Everyone brought something to help build God's house. And everyone shared in the workload. It would have taken years for the project had the people not worked together. It is amazing what we can do when God's people work together. God wants us to cooperate and work with each other. Let your child know God is pleased when we share and work well with others.

Home Connections

These items were used during the Bible story lesson and might be commonly found in your home. When your child sees or plays with one of the items mentioned below, help make the connection to the Bible story.

Tent: The children built different tents using various materials. You might wish to use a blanket and some chairs to build a tent. Talk about how people in Bible times gathered at the tabernacle, which basically was a tent, to worship God. Remind them of how the people in the Bible story worked together to build the tabernacle for God.

Colorful Cereal: Once the tabernacle was built, the people brought gifts to show God how much they loved him. In the lesson today, the children used colorful cereal to represent the gifts that were shared with God. Talk about how God wants us to share with others.

Keeping Connected

Here are two simple activities that were used in class during the Bible story lesson of Tabernacle Togetherness. Use these activities to help your child remember the Bible story lesson.

Cooperate! *(Song/Finger Play)*
Sing to the tune of "Jesus Loves Me."

> *Moms and dads and good friends too,*
> *can help me when there's work to do.*
> *I help, they help, it's just great!*
> *God helps us co-op-er-ate.*

Let's Build a Tabernacle
Have your child help you stack blocks to build the walls of the tabernacle. Then drape paper or cloth over the top as the tent-like roof. As you work, repeat, "Let's build a tabernacle, everyone help out. Share our things and share the work, then let's all scream and shout!"

Pile on the Prayer

(National Day of Prayer)

BIBLE STORY:
Daniel in the
Lions' Den
Daniel 6

BIBLE TRUTH:
Prayer is very
important to God.

BIBLE VERSE:
Are any of you
in trouble? Then
you should pray.
(James 5:13a)

Most children ages three to five are gaining awareness of the power of language. Typically, they are talking up a storm. During these years, some children also discover they have fears. Teach your little ones that in times of trouble, they can talk to God. There is unimaginable power in talking with God.

- In this lesson, children will **hear** the amazing story of Daniel in the lions' den, and how the power of prayer delivered him from his troubles.

- In this lesson, children will **learn** that prayer is important to God. God invites us and wants us to talk to him.

- In this lesson, children will **remember** that in times of trouble they should pray.

Lesson Five Snapshot

Get List:

- [ ] 1 copy of the *Hold'em-Up* reproducible (page 42) per child
- [ ] Scissors
- [ ] Crayons or markers
- [ ] Paper
- [ ] Tape
- [ ] Assorted phones
- [ ] Optional: Picture of Jesus
- [ ] Poster board or tag board
- [ ] Index cards
- [ ] Music CD
- [ ] CD player
- [ ] Animal crackers
- [ ] Plates
- [ ] Craft sticks
- [ ] Canned frosting
- [ ] Bible
- [ ] Paws from the Bible Story Link option in *Round'em-Up*
- [ ] Stickers
- [ ] 1 copy of *Home Connections* (page 47) for each child

The Heart of the Story:

Daniel was surrounded by circumstances that could have easily led to despair. As a youngster he was captured, taken far from his home, then separated from his family and conscripted into the king's service. He was surrounded by evil and eventually came under personal attack. But through it all, he remained faithful. He consistently talked with God about the circumstances. God listened and responded.

No matter what our age, we can face some pretty overwhelming circumstances too. Discover the peace and comfort God gives when we talk with him, and then share your experience of talking with God.

Hold'em-Up
Bible Story Reproducible Page

* 1 copy of the reproducible on this page for each child
* Scissors
* Crayons or markers

Copy the reproducible prayer mat and cut it out for each child. Have the children color their prayer mats and add a picture of themselves or others praying. As the children work, remind them they can always pray to God. When they are finished, fold up on the dotted lines, then put a knee on each side to pray.

FOLD FORWARD

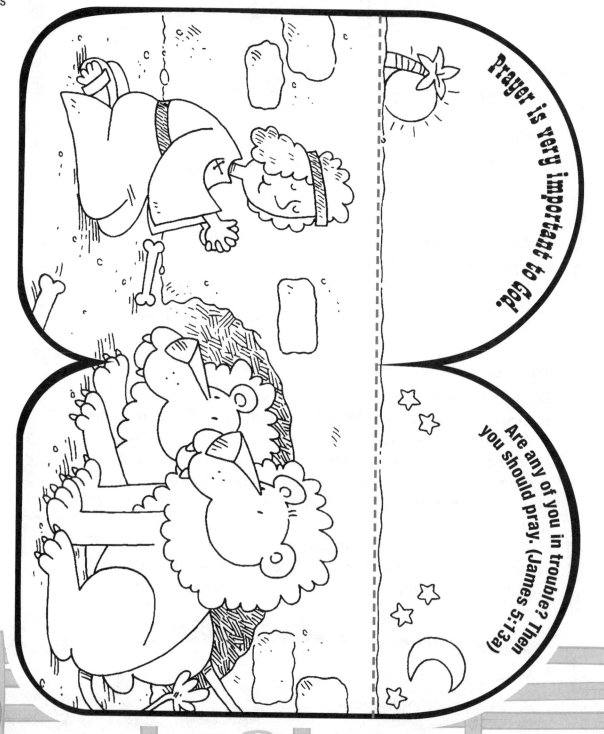

Prayer is very important to God.

Are any of you in trouble? Then you should pray. (James 5:13a)

Round'em-Up

Use these *Round'em-Up* activities to gather the children or anytime you need a quick group activity for a transition or filler.

Pile on the Prayer

★ Paper
★ Scissors

Help the children cut paper in the shape of lions' paws. Gather the children and have them tell you about things that scare them. Write their responses on the paws.

Spread the paws on the floor. Talk about how God wants us to pray all the time and especially when we are scared or in trouble. When you say, "Pile on the prayers," have the children find a paw to kneel on. Then have everyone say, "God listens to our prayers." Repeat and have the children kneel on different paws each time.

God Will Listen

Sing to the tune of "She'll Be Coming 'Round the Mountain."

God will listen to your prayers when you pray.
God will listen to your prayers when you pray.
If you ever are in trouble,
God will help you on the double.
God will listen to your prayers when you pray.

Morning, Noon or Night

★ 3 sheets of paper
★ Tape
★ Marker

On each piece of paper, draw one of the following: a sun coming up for morning, a full sun for noon and a moon for night. Tape each piece of paper to a different wall or part of the room. Tell the children that Daniel prayed three times a day: morning, noon and night. Then point out your sign for each. Tell the children that when you shout out a time of day, they must go to that sign. Then shout out, **Daniel prayed in the _____.** (Insert morning, noon or night.) Continue shouting out different times of the day. You might also tell the children how to go to each sign: walk, hop, crawl, etc., or vary your statement, for example, **We** (or children's names) **can pray in the _____.**

Lion Charades

Have the children show you what lions do when they are sleeping, when they are happy, when someone comes in their cage, when they are loving, when they are hungry and when they are angry. Talk about how God protected Daniel from the lions.

Bible Story
Hands-on Activities

These activities work well for large or small groups of children, or as stations, to introduce and/or reinforce the Bible story.

Talk to God

- Assorted phones
- Optional: Picture of Jesus

Children can understand that prayer is simply talking to God. We can talk to God in different ways because God is always with us and always hears us. And so, while bowing our heads, closing our eyes, folding our hands and kneeling are good behaviors when we pray, they are not the focus of our prayer and not necessarily required to pray because we can pray anytime. Provide different types of phones for the children to talk to God, just as they would talk to family members or friends. We can talk to God about anything. Put up a picture of Jesus to remind the children who they are talking with when praying.

Praying Hands

- Poster board or tag board
- Scissors
- Marker

Fold a piece of poster board in half to the size of standard copy paper. Have the children spread one hand on the poster board with the thumb aligned with the fold. Trace their hand. Then cut out around the hand, but do not cut along the part that is on the fold. When cut out, the hands will stand. Have the children draw things they would like to pray about or help them write ideas. You might also write the Bible Verse on one of the sides.

Bible Memory

Are any of you in trouble? Then you should pray. (James 5:13a)

- Index cards
- Markers
- Music CD
- CD Player

Use as many index cards as children. On one-third of the cards write a capital T. Place all cards facedown in a line or circle. Play the music; have the children step on the cards. When the music stops, the children pick up the cards they are on. Say, **Are any of you in trouble?** If they have a T on their card, they are in trouble! Then ask the children, **What should you do?** Have them respond with, "You should pray." Have the children with Ts get on their knees. Then have everyone get back on their feet, put the cards down and play again.

Pile It On

- Animal crackers
- Plates
- Craft sticks
- Canned frosting

In the Bible story, we'll learn how Daniel faces big trouble with some lions. When Daniel was in trouble, he prayed to God. Let's pretend this frosting is like prayer. We want to pile it on our trouble (lions). When you have troubles, remember to pile on the prayer to God. Let the children use craft sticks to pile frosting on their animal crackers. It's okay if everyone doesn't have a lion animal cracker. Who would want to be in a den with any of these wild animals? *Note: Check with parents for any food allergies children may have.*

Bible Story Time

* Bible
* Completed *Hold'em-Up* for each child (see page 42)

Gather your children for Story Time; be sure all the children have their *Hold'em-Ups* ready to go. **You're going to use your prayer mats to help me tell the Bible story. Whenever you hear the words "pray," "prayer" or "praying," kneel on your prayer mat briefly and then sit down again.** Have the children practice kneeling on their mats and then sitting down again. Use the Bible Verse for practice. Hold up a Bible for the children to see.

In the Bible, there is a book called Daniel, and this Bible story is about the man named Daniel.

Daniel loved God very much. Daniel knew that God wants us to <u>pray</u> *(kneel)* **to him. So Daniel <u>prayed</u>** *(kneel)* **to God three times a day—morning, noon and night. When Daniel <u>prayed</u>** *(kneel)***, he would always kneel to <u>pray</u>** *(kneel)***.**

One day, a confused king made a silly law. He said that people could not <u>pray</u> *(kneel)* **to God. Anyone who <u>prayed</u>** *(kneel)* **to God would be in big trouble. They would be thrown into a den of hungry lions.**

This new law made Daniel very sad, because Daniel knew that he would never stop <u>praying</u> *(kneel)* **to God. Daniel continued to <u>pray</u>** *(kneel)* **to God three times a day, morning, noon and night. Because Daniel was breaking the law, some mean men had Daniel arrested and threw him into a lions' den.**

Daniel was in trouble. What was Daniel going to do? That's right— Daniel began to <u>pray</u> *(kneel)***. Daniel <u>prayed</u>** *(kneel)* **and <u>prayed</u>** *(kneel)* **and <u>prayed</u>** *(kneel)***. God listened to Daniel and protected Daniel from the scary lions. God will listen to your <u>prayers</u>** *(kneel)* **too. God wants you to <u>pray</u>** *(kneel)* **to him. When you are in trouble, you can <u>pray</u>** *(kneel)* **to God too. You can always <u>pray</u>** *(kneel)* **to God. He is always listening to your <u>prayers</u>** *(kneel)***.**

* **Who did not stop praying to God?** *(Daniel)*
* **When can you pray to God?** *(morning, noon, night, anytime)*
* **Who is always listening when you pray?** *(God, because prayer is important to God)*

Send'em-Off

- Paws from Bible Story Link
- Stickers
- Completed *Hold'em-Up* for each child

Teacher Tip

God listens to our prayers and always responds. This doesn't mean his response is always what we expect or want, but it is always good. Focus on how God never leaves us in times of trouble. He will surely help us through the difficult times if he chooses not to remove our difficulties.

Itty Bitty Bible Facts

Lions were greatly feared by the people during Daniel's time. It was considered the cruelest of punishments to be fed to the lions. It was almost always certain death with no way of escape. Imagine facing that situation armed only with powerful prayer!

Prayer

Ask the children to name troubles God can help them with. Or use the paws from the Bible Story Link in *Round'em-Up*. Talk about how we can pray to God to help us with any problem or trouble. Lead the children in this prayer: **Dear God, thank you for your help so dear. Thank you for your listening ear. In Jesus' name, amen.**

Cleanup

Ask the children to pretend to be lions as they clean up the room, roaring as they work. Tell them that when you say, **Prayer is important to God,** they should clean quietly as you tell them additional interesting points of the Bible story, such as how God used an angel to close the mouths of the lions and that Daniel spent an entire night in the den.

Homeward Bound

As the children leave, make sure they have their completed *Hold'em-Ups* they made for Bible Story Time. As the children leave, put a sticker on one of their knees. Tell them that the sticker should remind them that Daniel kneeled when he prayed to God.

- **When can you pray to God?**
- **What does the sticker remind you of?**

Home Connections

It's a Snap!

Title: Pile on the Prayer (National Day of Prayer)

Bible Story: Daniel in the Lions' Den
Daniel 6

Bible Truth: Prayer is very important to God.

Bible Verse: Are any of you in trouble? Then you should pray. (James 5:13a)

- In this lesson, your child **heard** the amazing story of Daniel in the lions' den, and how the power of prayer delivered him from his troubles.

- In this lesson, your child **learned** that prayer is important to God. God invites us and wants us to talk to him.

- In this lesson, your child **remembered** that in times of trouble they should pray.

Daniel was a man whose lifeline was talking with God. When you are in trouble who do you talk with? Who is your lifeline? Do you go to God first and ask him what to do? God is there for us no matter what time of day and no matter what the situation. God wants nothing more than for us to talk with him and be in constant communication with him. Prayer is not only important to us, but it is important to God, too. He wants us to tell him what is on our hearts and minds. Teach your little one to talk with God at all times.

Home Connections

These items listed were used during the Bible story lessons and might be commonly found in your home. When your child sees or plays with one of the items mentioned below, help make the connection to the Bible story.

Phones: The children learned that praying is simply talking with God. When you notice that your child needs to talk about something, pull out a picture of Jesus and a phone. Have your child sit and chat on the phone with Jesus. Use the picture so they know who they are talking to. Remind your child that God listens to our prayers at all times.

Knees, Hands and Eyes: People pray in many different ways. Talk about how people eat using different things such as spoons, forks, knives, plates, etc. Talk about how people pray differently too. Some kneel on the ground. Some people fold their hands when they pray. And some people close their eyes. All of these are different ways to pray.

Keeping Connected

Here's a simple activity from the Bible story lesson, Pile on the Prayers. Use this to help your child remember the Bible story lesson.

God Will Listen *(Song/Finger Play)*
Sing to the tune of "She'll Be Coming 'Round the Mountain."

God will listen to your prayers when you pray.
God will listen to your prayers when you pray.
If you ever are in trouble, God will help you on the double.
God will listen to your prayers when you pray.

Prayer
Ask your child about things that God can help with. Talk about how he or she can pray to God for help with any problem or trouble. Then lead her in this prayer: **Dear God, thank you for your help so dear. Thank you for your listening ear. In Jesus' name, amen.**

Joy, Joy, Joy

(Christmas)

BIBLE STORY:

Jesus' Birth
Luke 2:1–20

BIBLE TRUTH:

Jesus the Savior
is born.

BIBLE VERSE:

A Savior has been
born to you. He is
Christ the Lord.
(Luke 2:11)

Children ages three to five are full of excitement, anticipation and joy knowing that Christmas is here. Help the children "unwrap" the real reason for all the joy of the season—Jesus our Savior has been born!

⭐ In this lesson, children will **hear** the joyful story of the humble birth of Jesus.

⭐ In this lesson, children will **learn** that Jesus, who is our Savior, was born a little baby in a stable.

⭐ In this lesson, children will **remember** a Savior has been born, and he is Christ the Lord.

Lesson Six Snapshot

Get List:

- [ ] 1 copy of the *Hold'em-Up* reproducible on page 50 per child
- [ ] Scissors
- [ ] Crayons and markers
- [ ] Glue
- [ ] Yarn
- [ ] Large box
- [ ] Newspaper
- [ ] Masking tape
- [ ] Jump rope
- [ ] CD player
- [ ] Christmas music CD
- [ ] Doll

- [ ] Baby items
- [ ] Box or manger from *Round'em-Up* Bible Story Link
- [ ] Stuffed animals
- [ ] Building blocks
- [ ] Plastic animals
- [ ] Bible
- [ ] Robe
- [ ] Microwave safe bowl, spoon
- [ ] 1 cup butterscotch chips
- [ ] ½ cup milk chocolate chips

- [ ] Pkg. of chow mein noodles
- [ ] Waxed paper
- [ ] Optional: Orange marshmallow circus peanuts
- [ ] Box or manger
- [ ] Drinking straws
- [ ] Basket or manger
- [ ] Flashlight
- [ ] Chenille wire
- [ ] 1 copy of *Home Connections* (page 55) for each child

The Heart of the Story:

This story brings a smile to our faces, lifts our spirits and leads us to eternal joy because of the one who was born and his gift of salvation to us.

You'll share a simple story with profound meaning and impact for all people and all time. The children you teach may not understand all the impact now, but you can help them learn to love the story. That will help set it into their hearts and minds as part of the spiritual foundation for receiving salvation when they're ready. Let the joy begin!

Hold'em-Up
Bible Story Reproducible Page

Before class, copy and then cut out the mouse mask and its eye holes for each child. Cut yarn into two-inch pieces. Have the children color their mouse masks. Then hand each child six pieces of string to glue onto the face of the mouse for whiskers. Children will hold up their masks to their faces using the ears.

- ✦ 1 copy of the reproducible on this page for each child
- ✦ Scissors
- ✦ Crayons or markers
- ✦ Glue
- ✦ Yarn

Jesus the Savior is born.

A Savior has been born to you. He is Christ the Lord. (Luke 2:11)

Round'em-Up

Use theses *Round'em-Up* activities to gather the children or anytime you need a quick group activity for a transition or filler.

What's a Manger?

Have the children sit around a large open box that will serve as a manger. Talk about how a manger is a feeding trough for animals. Have the children help you tear strips of paper into your manger as pretend food. You might have the children name animals that would eat from a manger as they toss the paper into the manger box. This manger could be used later for Babies Bring Joy in the Hands-on Activities.

Bible Story Link
- Large box
- Newspaper

Jump for Joy

Mark a large circle on the floor using masking tape. Crouch in the center of the circle holding one end of the jump rope. Have the children stand but spread out inside the circle. As the music plays, spin around bringing the jumprope around the circle just above the floor for the children to jump over as it passes under their feet.

Game
- Masking tape
- Jump rope
- CD player
- Christmas music CD

On The Night

Sing to the tune of "Old McDonald Had a Farm."

On the night that Jesus was born:
Joy, joy, joy, joy, joy.
And on that night, there was a __
(name an animal).
Joy, joy, joy, joy, joy.
With a __ __ (animal sound) here,
and a __ __ there, here a __ ,
there a __ , everywhere a __ __.
On the night that Jesus was born:
Joy, joy, joy, joy, joy!

Song/ Fingerplay

Feelings of Joy

Have the children demonstrate different facial expressions. Ask them a number of questions, and have them show you how people would react.

Show Me

- **How do people feel when they know they are going to have a baby?**
- **How do people feel when they are happy, joyful or excited?**
- **How do people feel when they get presents?**
- **How do people respond when they learn Jesus was born?**

Bible Story
Hands-on Activities

These activities work well for large or small groups of children, or as stations, to introduce and/or reinforce the Bible story.

Babies Bring Joy

* Doll
* Baby items
* Box or manger from Bible Story Link
* Stuffed animals

Tell the children how happy and joyful people are when a baby is born. Help the children arrange the materials you provide to represent how things might have been when Jesus was born. Children may play the parts of Mary, Joseph, shepherds and angels who were present. Celebrate his birth together.

Build a Stable

* Building blocks
* Plastic animals

Provide plastic animals and building blocks. Have the children build stables and place some animals inside each one. Talk about how Jesus was born with the animals because there were so many people at the town and there was no room for him to be born anywhere else. Besides Mary and Joseph, there were also shepherds and angels at the stable too.

Bible Memory

A Savior has been born to you. He is Christ the Lord. (Luke 2:11)

* Bible
* Robe

Tell the children you're going to pretend to be an angel. Put a robe on. Show the children the Bible. In the Bible an angel delivered a special message. Tell them they're going to help you deliver a special message. You shout out, **A Savior has been born to you.** And they reply by shouting out, "He is Christ the Lord." Repeat several times, each time getting louder and louder.

Manger Munchies

* Microwave-safe bowl
* Spoon
* 1 cup butterscotch chips
* ½ cup milk chocolate chips
* Pkg. of chow mein noodles
* Waxed paper
* Optional: Orange marshmallow circus peanuts

Microwave butterscotch chips and milk chocolate chips on medium power for 60 seconds. Stir, and if necessary, microwave an additional 15 seconds. Stir in one package of chow mein noodles. Spread out a sheet of waxed paper. Drop spoonfuls of the mixture onto the wax paper to make "mangers." You might add a marshmallow circus peanut to each manger to represent the baby in the manger. Allow to cool before eating. *Note: Check with parents for any food allergies children may have.*

Bible Story Time

Bible
Box or manger
Completed *Hold'em-Up* for each child (from the reproducible on page 50)

Teacher Tip

During Story Time, you may have children who don't want to stay in their spots. Use tape to mark an X for their spot, or give each child a carpet square to sit on. These types of boundaries help some children stay put, and it also helps them to keep their hands and feet to themselves.

Gather your children around a box or your manger from the Bible Story Link in *Round'em-Up*. Be sure they have their *Hold'em-Up* mouse masks. Have the children put their mouse masks to their faces and look through the eye holes.

Oh my! What are all of these mice doing here? You must be stable mice! Do you know what stable mice say? They say, "Joy, joy, joy!" Say that with me: joy, joy, joy. **When I point to you little stable mice, hold your mouse masks to your faces, look through the eye holes, and say, "Joy, joy, joy!" Let's give it a try.** Practice once or twice. **You are good stable mice, and we will have a joyful time as you help me tell our Bible story.** Hold up a Bible for the children to see.

A long time ago in a stable, there were little stable mice that lived with some cows and sheep. (point, act as if you are holding up your pretend mouse mask and lead the children saying, "Joy, joy, joy.") **One night some strangers came to the stable. Their names were Mary and Joseph. They had come from a town far away, and they were very tired from their long journey. They needed a place to rest, so all of the animals at the stable were excited and full of** (point etc.) **to have the new guests.**

That night the stable was suddenly filled with a bright light. There were angels all around singing (point etc.). **What was happening? What was all the excitement about? A baby boy had been born, and his name was Jesus. He was born right in the stable with the animals. His mother wrapped him in soft cloths and put him in the manger so he could sleep warm and comfortable.**

He was a special baby because he's the Savior of the world. His birth was wonderful and joyful news. The shepherds, the angels and even all of the animals were full of (point etc.). **You can be full of** (point etc.) **because Jesus our Savior was born** (point etc.). **Jesus was born on Christmas day.**

* **Who was born on Christmas day?** *(Jesus)*
* **Why was Jesus a special baby?** *(he is the Savior of the world)*
* **What can you be full of because Jesus was born?** *(joy)*

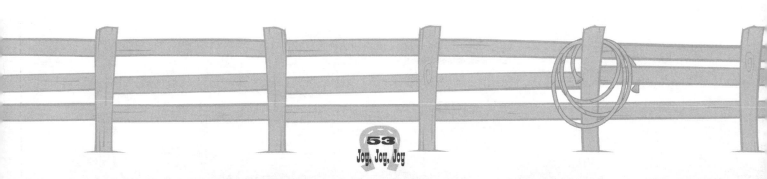

Send'em-Off

- Drinking straws
- Basket or box for a manger
- Flashlight
- Chenille wire
- Completed *Hold'em-Up* for each child

Prayer

Place drinking straws in a basket or the manger you made in the Bible Story Link during *Round'em-Up*. As the children take a straw from the manger, have them tell one thing that makes them full of joy. Then lead them in this prayer, **Dear Jesus, we love you, and we are glad you came as a baby on Christmas day a long time ago. Thank you for filling our hearts with joy. In Jesus' name, amen.**

Cleanup

Tell the children how a long time ago a great star shone in the sky to direct people to where baby Jesus was. Turn on your flashlight. Explain that you are going to shine your flashlight to direct them to things or areas that need to be cleaned up.

Homeward Bound

As the children leave, make sure they have their completed *Hold'em-Ups* they made for Bible Story Time. Also hand each child a chenille wire bent in the shape of the letter J. Tell them it can remind them of Jesus, the baby born in the manger, and for joy. Have the children tuck the end of the J behind them for their mouse tail!

- **What does the J stand for?**
- **Why are you full of joy?**

Home Connections

It's a Snap!

Title: Joy, Joy, Joy (Christmas)

Bible Story: Jesus' Birth
Luke 2:1–20

Bible Truth: Jesus the Savior is born.

Bible Verse: A Savior has been born to you. He is Christ the Lord. (Luke 2:11)

- In this lesson, your child **heard** the joyful story of the humble birth of Jesus.

- In this lesson, your child **learned** that Jesus, who is our Savior, was born a little baby in a stable.

- In this lesson, your child **remembered** a Savior has been born, and he is Christ the Lord.

Mary and Joseph were happy when Jesus was born. They were grateful that God had chosen them to be Jesus' earthly parents. The shepherds were scared, then excited and happy when they heard the angels' news. God's Son had come! Excitement filled the air. The long awaited birth of the Savior had finally arrived. Christmas is a special time each year when we celebrate the birth of Christ. Knowing Jesus gives us joy all year long. Share your joy with your little one throughout the whole year. Jesus our Savior is here!

Home Connections

These are items that were used during the Bible story lesson that might be commonly found in your home. When your child sees or plays with one of the items mentioned below, help make the connection to the Bible story.

Dolls: Dolls were used to explain how Jesus was born a baby a long time ago. Encourage your child to take care of the baby Jesus. Then talk about how baby Jesus grew into a boy and then a man.

Jump rope: During class, the children used a jump rope to practice jumping for joy. Use a jump rope with your child and talk about things that make you jump for joy. Talk about how Jesus brings us joy.

Animals on the farm (toys or pictures): Your child learned that Jesus was born in a place where animals lived. After Jesus was born, he was laid in a feeding trough for animals called a manger. Talk about how all this was in God's plan for Jesus. He was a special baby because he is God's Son.

Keeping Connected

Here are two simple activities that were used in class during the Bible story lesson of Joy, Joy, Joy. Use these activities to help your child remember the Bible story lesson.

Manger Munchies
Microwave one cup butterscotch chips and one-half cup milk chocolate chips on medium power until softened. Stir in one package chow mein noodles. Drop spoonfuls onto waxed paper and shape each one into a little manger. Then add a marshmallow circus peanut to each one, cool, and enjoy.

On The Night (*Song/Finger Play*)
Sing to the tune of "Old McDonald Had a Farm."
On the night that Jesus was born: Joy, joy, joy, joy, joy.
And on that night, there was a __(name an animal). Joy, joy, joy, joy, joy.
With a __ __ (animal sound) here, and a __ __ there, here a __ ,
there a __ , everywhere a __ __.
On the night that Jesus was born: Joy, joy, joy, joy, joy!

The Very Caring Friend

BIBLE STORY:
The Good Samaritan
Luke 10:29–37

BIBLE TRUTH:
God wants us to
care for others.

BIBLE VERSE:
Be kind and tender
to one another.
(Ephesians 4:32a)

Caring tends to be a natural trait expressed by most children ages three to five. Foster this trait as you teach the children that God wants us to care for others. Help them all become little Samaritans for Christ.

⭐ In this lesson, children will **hear** how one man stopped to care for a hurting man, even though other people passed him by.

⭐ In this lesson, children will **learn** that God wants us to care for others.

⭐ In this lesson, children will **remember** to be kind and tender to one another.

Lesson Seven Snapshot

Get List:

- ☐ 1 copy of the *Hold'em-Up* reproducible (page 58) per child
- ☐ Scissors
- ☐ Crayons and markers
- ☐ Tape
- ☐ Poster board
- ☐ Stick-on bandages
- ☐ Permanent marker
- ☐ Doll
- ☐ Masking tape
- ☐ Various toys, ball or beanbags
- ☐ Building blocks and other construction toys
- ☐ Plastic animals (donkeys) and characters
- ☐ Construction paper
- ☐ Glue sticks
- ☐ Pair of sandals
- ☐ Paper plates
- ☐ Sliced bananas, strawberries and kiwi
- ☐ Bible
- ☐ 1 copy of *Home Connections* (page 63) for each child

The Heart of the Story:

This Bible story is about *be*-friending everyone around us no matter who those people are. It requires careful thought, leading to action that is kind and tender.

It is not an easy lesson to implement. In fact, the story shows that most people don't! Focus on the one who gets it right. Strive to be like the Samaritan, especially when personal difference, historic ill-will, or cultural conflict might nudge you to *de*-friend people. It only takes a little act of kindness to make a difference for someone.

Hold'em-Up

Bible Story Reproducible Page

- ☀ 1 copy of the reproducible on this page for each child
- ☀ Scissors
- ☀ Crayons or markers
- ☀ Tape

Copy the reproducible for each child and cut along the outer edges. Cut between the squares and around the middle sections. Children should color the pictures. Fold forward on the broken lines. Tape the tab to the back of the stop sign to form a pop-up in the round.

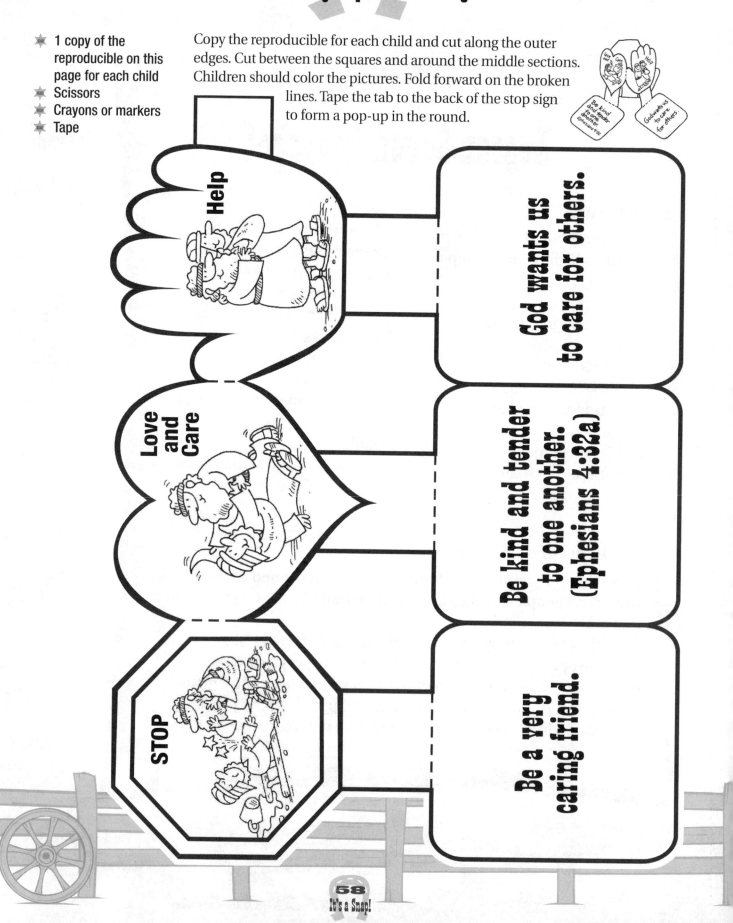

Help

Love and Care

STOP

God wants us to care for others.

Be kind and tender to one another. (Ephesians 4:32a)

Be a very caring friend.

Round'em-Up

Use these *Round'em-Up* activities to gather the children or anytime you need a quick group activity for a transition or filler.

Bible Story Link

* Poster board
* Stick-on bandages
* Permanent marker

A Big Hurt

Before class, cut poster board to make a giant stick doll. In class, talk about ways people get hurt, including how our hearts can be hurt in different ways than our bodies. Write the wounds you talk about on stick-on bandages. Have the children stick the bandages on your doll. Tell the children the Bible story is about a caring friend who helped a hurting man. Explain how they can care for others too.

Song/Fingerplay

A Little Man Went Walking

Sing to the tune of "Little Bunny Foo Foo."

A little man went walking, down a dusty road.
(hold up one finger)
Along came some robbers, and bonked him on the head.
(slap top of seat with palm)
   (Spoken) *Then came a religious man and he said ...*
(Sing) *I see you're injured, I'm not going to help you.* (shake finger no)
I will keep on walking and leave you there alone. (swing arms)
   (Spoken) *Then came a lawyer man and he said…*
(Sing) *I see you're injured, I'm too busy to help you.* (shake finger no)
I will keep on walking and leave you there alone. (swing arms)
   (Spoken) *Then came a caring man and he said…*
(Sing) *You are very injured; I am here to help you.* (point to self)
I will help you up and be your friend today.
(make a scooping motion and clasp hands together)

Game

* Doll
* Masking tape

Good-Friend Race

Make a masking tape starting line. Have the children form a line behind the tape. Place the doll about 10 feet away. Have the first child in line run to the doll, tag it and then return to take the hand of the next child in line to run together and tag the doll. Have the children continue running and adding another child until all are joined. The last child picks up the doll and everyone shouts, "We're good friends!"

Show Me

* Various toys, ball or beanbags

Caring Friends

Have the children find a partner. Tell the children they will eventually be partners with everyone. Hand a toy to each pair. Have them show you how they can carry their toy for five steps together using only one hand. Then have them show you using no hands. Repeat with different partners.

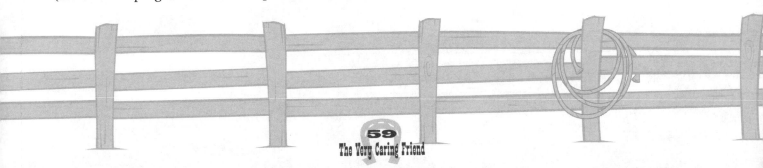

Bible Story
Hands-on Activities

These activities work well for large or small groups of children, or as stations, to introduce and/or reinforce the Bible story.

Activity 1

Traveling Down a Dusty Road

* Building blocks and construction toys
* Plastic animals (donkeys) and characters

Let the children use building blocks and other toys to make roads. Set up plastic animals, especially donkeys, and other characters to travel the roads. Talk about how some Bible time people rode donkeys, but many walked everywhere they went.

Activity 2

Heart to Heart

* Construction paper
* Scissors
* Glue sticks

Cut several hearts of different sizes and colors from construction paper. Have the children glue hearts together as collages. You might have the children combine their heart-collages into one large creation. We do and say things to be kind and caring but those words and actions come from our hearts. Combining our hearts together can lead to a lot of kindness!

Activity 3

Bible Memory

Be kind and tender to one another. (Ephesians 4:32a)

* Pair of sandals

Have the children sit in a circle facing inward. Show the children a pair of sandals. Explain that people in Bible times wore sandals, not shoes. Walk around the circle and hand the sandals to one child. When you hand the sandals over say, "Be kind and tender to one another." Have that child put the sandals on and walk around the outside of the circle one complete time. Then have that child hand the sandals to another child, repeating the Bible Verse with each handoff. Then have that child sit down facing outward. Continue until all the children have had a turn.

Activity 4

Stoplight Friends

* Paper plates
* Sliced bananas, strawberries and kiwi

Tell the children we want to be caring and help others like the man in the Bible story. Have the children place a slice of each kind of fruit on their plates to resemble traffic lights. Talk about how the "yellow" fruit (light) can remind you to **look** for people who are hurting. The "green" fruit (light) can remind you to **go** to people when they need help. The "red" fruit (light) can remind you to **stop** and help. We can all learn to help and care for others; we can be "stoplight friends." *Note: Check with parents for any food allergies children may have.*

Bible Story Time

* Bible
* Completed *Hold'em-Up* for each child (made from page 58)

As you gather your children for Story Time, be sure they have their *Hold'em-Ups* ready to go. During your Bible storytelling, have the children show you the part of their *Hold'em-Ups* that matches the underlined words in the story. Hold up a Bible for the children to see.

The Bible has a story Jesus told about a traveler, some robbers and three men. Only one of the men was a friend to the traveler. Listen to find out who was a friend for the traveler.

A man was riding his donkey along a dusty road going from one town to another, when suddenly he was attacked by a group of robbers. The robbers beat him up and took all of his money. They left the man lying on the side of the road. He was hurt very badly and could not move. The man needed someone to lend him a helping <u>hand</u>.

A while later a religious man came walking down the road. He saw the hurt traveler. But he did not <u>stop</u> to help. He kept on walking right past him.

Was this religious man a friend to the traveler? *(no, a friend would help)* The traveler's <u>heart</u> was very sad. God was not pleased either because he wants us to care for others.

After a while a lawyer came walking down the road. He saw the hurt traveler too. But he was too busy to <u>stop</u> and give the hurting traveler a helping <u>hand</u>. Once again the traveler's <u>heart</u> was very sad. Was the lawyer a friend to the traveler? *(no, a friend would help)*

This poor traveler was hurting and needed help. People were not being very friendly toward him. Then came along another man from a different country. This one was riding a donkey. This man also saw that the traveler lying on the side of the road was hurt. He <u>stopped</u> and got off his donkey. He used his helping <u>hands</u> to help the hurting traveler. The traveler's <u>heart</u> was so happy. Someone finally <u>stopped</u> to be his friend.

Was the man on the donkey a friend to the traveler? Yes he was. A friend will be kind and tender to others. A friend will be very caring. A friend will <u>stop</u> and use their helping <u>hands</u> to make happy <u>hearts</u>. God wants you to be a friend to others. God wants you to care for others.

* **What does God want us to do?** *(God wants us to care for others)*
* **Who was kind and caring toward the man who was hurt?** *(the man who stopped and helped)*
* **How can you care for others?**

Send'em-Off

- Construction paper
- Scissors
- Marker
- Completed *Hold'em-Up* for each child
- Stick-on bandages

Teacher Tip

Privately and gently, but still firmly, ask bossy children to be in charge of themselves, not others. In private conversation, you might repeat their words and tone of voice helping them hear how they sound. An alternative for stubborn and insistent children is asking them to point out to you what others should do.

Itty Bitty Bible Facts

The Good Samaritan gave money to the innkeeper to pay in advance for the hurt man's care. The amount he gave equaled what he would have earned working for two days. That was a lot of money to give for someone who was not only a stranger, but also part of a group of people who most other people looked down upon and did not treat well.

Prayer

Before class, cut a large heart shape from paper. Ask the children the names of their friends. Write their responses on the paper. Then lead the children in this prayer: **Dear God, thank you for all our friends. Thank you for** (read the names)**. Help us to be kind and caring toward our friends. In Jesus' name, amen.**

Cleanup

Tell the children that in the Bible story, we learned that friends help each other. Have the children find a friend and lock elbows. Then each pair of friends work together to clean up your room. Remind the children to care for each other, being kind and gentle.

Homeward Bound

As the children leave, make sure they have their completed *Hold'em-Ups* they made for Bible Story Time. Hand a bandage to each child just before leaving. Tell them the bandage can remind them to care for others, and especially people who hurt.

- **What does the bandage remind you of?**
- **Tell me the names of two of your friends.**

Home Connections

It's a Snap!

Title: The Very Caring Friend

Bible Story: The Good Samaritan *Luke 10:29–37*

Bible Truth: God wants us to care for others.

Bible Verse: Be kind and tender to one another. (Ephesians 4:32a)

- In this lesson, your child **heard** how one man stopped to care for a hurting man, even though other people passed him by.

- In this lesson, your child **learned** that God wants us to care for others.

- In this lesson, your child **remembered** to be kind and tender to one another.

Friendships can develop during all the times of our lives, but it may be when we are hurt that our best friends emerge. Painful times may also be some of the best for showing our care and concern for our friends—not because we want to be seen as a best friend but because this is the kind of care Jesus asks us to demonstrate. It is the same for your young children, just adapted to their level of experience and understanding. Help your child recognize that we can treat everyone as if he or she is our friend.

Home Connections

These are items that were used during the Bible story lesson that might be commonly found in your home. When your child sees or plays with one of the items mentioned below, help make the connection to the Bible story.

Traffic light: Although this may not be found in your home, it is typically seen throughout a day spent in a car. In the Bible lesson, your child was taught to look for people who are hurting (yellow), go to others and be friends (green), and to stop and help each other (red).

Bandages: Bandages were used to talk about the hurts that people have. In the Bible story, the very good friend stopped to help a hurting man. Talk about things that hurt your child. Talk about physical and emotional pain. Then remind your child that God wants us to be a friend to others who may be hurting.

Keeping Connections

Here is a simple activity that was used in class during the Bible story lesson of The Very Caring Friend. Use these activities to help your child remember the Bible story lesson.

Traveling Down a Dusty Road

Use building blocks and other toys to make roads. Set up plastic animals, especially donkeys, and other characters to travel the roads. Talk about how some Bible-time people rode donkeys, but many walked everywhere they went.

Prayer

Cut out a large heart shape. Write the names of your child's friends on the heart. Then lead your child in this prayer: **"Dear God, thank you for all my friends. Thank you for _____ (read the names). Help me to be kind and caring toward my friends. In Jesus' name, amen.**

God Is Full of Love

(Valentine's Day)

BIBLE STORY:
Prodigal Son
Luke 15:11–32

BIBLE TRUTH:
God loves and
forgives us. God
loves everyone.

BIBLE VERSE:
Great is his love for
us. (Psalm 117:2a)

Unconditional loves means that God loves us no matter what we do—the good, the bad and the ugly. Young children are very accepting of love. Show them how God wants to fill their hearts with his overflowing love.

★ In this lesson, children will **hear** how a father loved and forgave his son, who made bad choices.

★ In this lesson, children will **learn** that, like the father, God loves and forgives us, no matter what choices we make.

★ In this lesson, children will **remember** God has a great amount of love for us.

Lesson Eight Snapshot

Get List:

- [ ] 1 copy of the *Hold'em-Up* reproducible (page 66) per child
- [ ] Scissors
- [ ] Tape
- [ ] Crayons and markers
- [ ] Red and white paper
- [ ] Large sheets of paper
- [ ] Tape
- [ ] Suitcase
- [ ] Poster board
- [ ] Paper
- [ ] Colored paper
- [ ] Glue
- [ ] Heart-suit cards from 3 decks of playing cards
- [ ] Tissue paper
- [ ] Bible
- [ ] Heart-shaped cookie cutter
- [ ] Sliced bread
- [ ] Jelly
- [ ] Craft sticks
- [ ] 2 large sheets craft foam
- [ ] 1 copy of *Home Connections* (page 71) for each child

The Heart of the Story:

A father never stopped loving his child —and even ran to embrace him— despite how old his child was and what he had done. Our very heavenly father thinks and acts exactly the same with us. Age and actions will never cause God to redefine his love for us, withhold his forgiveness or stop running after us.

Children around four years old are concrete thinkers and tend to think our love for them might hinge on how well they behave. Your consistent love, shown through acceptance and forgiveness, helps them learn the truth about God's great love for each of them.

Hold'em-Up

Bible Story Reproducible Page

- 1 copy of the reproducible on this page for each child
- Scissors
- Crayons or markers
- Tape

Copy and cut out the reproducible pieces below for each child. Cut the slits on the large heart. Tape the strips together where indicated to form one long Bible story strip. Have the children color the heart and the pictures on the Bible story strip. Insert the strip through the back side of the top slit in the heart, then from front to back through the lower slit. Pull down on the strip to show each frame as you tell the Bible story.

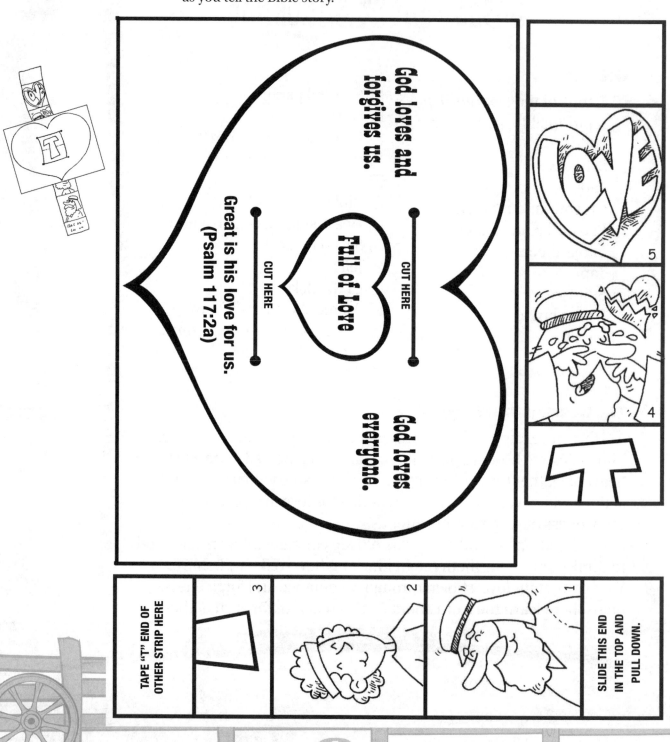

Full of Love

God loves and forgives us.

Great is his love for us. (Psalm 117:2a)

CUT HERE

God loves everyone.

5

4

TAPE "T" END OF OTHER STRIP HERE

3

2

1

SLIDE THIS END IN THE TOP AND PULL DOWN.

Round'em-Up

Use the *Round'em-Up* activities to gather the children or anytime you need a quick group activity for a transition or filler.

Bible Story Link

* Scissors
* Red and white paper
* Large sheet of paper
* Tape

Find a Heart

Before class, cut hearts from red and white paper and hide them around the room. During class, gather the children and show them a paper heart. Ask, **What does a heart remind you of?** Reinforce *love* and *acceptance*. Have the children find the hearts and collect them. When they are finished, tape the hearts to a special place on a wall or on a large piece of paper on a wall, as a reminder of all the love they found.

Game

* Paper
* Scissors
* Suitcase

Full of Love

Before class, cut out paper hearts and place them in a suitcase. In class, gather the children around your closed suitcase. Tell them this suitcase reminds you of when someone packs up their things to leave home. But then it's opened when we return home. This suitcase is packed full of love. Open the suitcase and spill the hearts all around the room. Challenge the children to pack the hearts into the suitcase as fast as they can. When they are finished, have them shout, "God is packed full of love for you!" Have the children point to someone on the "you." Repeat.

Song/ Fingerplay

God Loves Us

Sing to the tune of "Three Blind Mice."

God loves us; God loves us.
Great is his love; great is his love.
He loves us more than we can know.
He loves us from our heads to our toes.
God loves us; God loves us.

Show Me

* Poster board
* Marker
* Paper hearts in nine different colors, two of each color
* Glue
* Tape

Hearts Match

Before class, create a large heart on poster board. Draw heavy lines dividing the heart into nine sections. Cut out pairs of hearts in nine different colors. Glue one of each color in the nine sections of your large heart.

In class, give children the nine colored hearts with tape. Have them match the colors so they tape their hearts in the corresponding sections of the large heart. Talk about how hearts remind us of love.

Bible Story
Hands-on-Activities

These activities work well for large or small groups of children, or as stations, to introduce and/or reinforce the Bible story.

Activity 1

Heart to Heart

* Heart-suit cards from 3 decks of playing cards

Point out the hearts on your cards. Talk about how hearts remind us of love and God's love for us. Show how the cards can be used to build and stack, then let the children experiment. You might spread the number cards face-side-up and let the children collect matching sets.

Activity 2

A Heart Full of Love

* Large sheet of paper
* Tissue paper
* Scissors
* Glue

Cut out one large heart. Cut tissue paper into one-inch squares. Show the children the paper heart. **This paper heart reminds me of love. But this heart is empty. We need to fill up this heart because God's heart is full of love for us. Let's make a heart that is full of love!** Have the children glue tissue paper squares onto the heart. When the heart is finished, have the children say, "God's heart is full of love."

Activity 3

Bible Memory

Great is his love for us. (Psalm 117:2a)

* Bible
* Paper
* Scissors
* Marker

Cut out seven large hearts. Write a word and the reference of the Bible verse on each heart. Show the children each heart in verse order as you say each word for the children. Repeat, but have the children say each word with you. Repeat with the children. When they have learned the verse, turn one heart to show the blank backside of the heart but still say the entire verse correctly, replacing the missing word. Continue until all the hearts are turned to the blank side.

Activity 4

A Little Taste of Love

* Heart-shaped cookie cutter
* Sliced bread
* Jelly
* Craft sticks

Use a cookie cutter to cut heart shapes from sliced bread. Talk about how hearts remind you of love. Have the children use the craft sticks to spread a little "love" (jelly) on their hearts. Talk about how God wants to spread his love to everyone. *Note: Check with parents for any food allergies children may have.*

Bible Story Time

- ⭐ Bible
- ⭐ Completed *Hold'em-Up* for each child (from page 66)

Gather your children with their *Hold'em-Ups*. Demonstrate how to slide the Bible story strip down to show each frame on the heart. Stop at each picture and point out the frame numbers. Let the children practice. Have the children pull up to show picture 1. Tell them to listen for the picture numbers as you tell the Bible story. Hold up a Bible for the children to see.

God loves everyone, no matter what we do, good or bad. Jesus told a story to help us understand this. The hearts with the picture strips that you made can help tell that story.

There was a man. We see that man in the first picture. Everyone look at the picture of the man in your heart. This man is the father and he loves his son very much.

Pull your Bible story strip down to picture 2. This is a picture of the father's son. The boy lived at home with his father. He was a good boy; he went to school and worked very hard.

Pull your Bible story strip down to picture 3 showing the letter *T*. This is the letter *T*. *T* stands for trouble. One day the boy decided to pack up his things and leave home. He asked his father for a lot of money, and his father gave it to the boy. The boy went away and made some very bad choices. The boy got into a lot of trouble wasting the money on bad things.

Pull the Bible story strip down to picture 4. Who is in this fourth picture? *(the picture looks like the father and there is a broken heart, too)* **What is the father doing?** *(he is crying, he looks sad)* **The father was sad that his son left home and was making bad choices. The father's heart broke because his son was in trouble, but the father still loved his son very much.**

Pull the Bible story strip down to picture 5. The picture shows a heart full of love. The word *LOVE*, L-O-V-E, is inside the heart and fills it completely. The son made some wrong choices and his father was sad, but the father still loved his son very much. The father's heart was full of love for his son, no matter what the son did. The father forgave his son for making bad choices and wasting all his money because the father loved his son so much.

God is just like the father in this story. No matter what we do, God loves us and forgives us. God loves everyone.

- ⭐ **Who loves you?** *(God)*
- ⭐ **What does God do when you do something bad?** *(he loves me and forgives me)*

Send'em-Off

* Red paper
* Scissors
* 2 large sheets of craft foam
* Completed *Hold'em-Up* for each child (from page 66)

Teacher Tip

It's a challenge to discipline yet assure the disciplined child of our love. God does it well, just as he does all things. He speaks the truth clearly and simply in love, and stays connected emotionally both during and after. For us that can mean making short and direct statements in a normal tone and volume. Then staying involved, inviting the one disciplined to join us in activities and adventures.

Itty Bitty Bible Facts

Pigs were considered "unclean" so Jews could not eat them. In fact, they weren't allowed to even touch them. The son had done one of the worst, most horrible things imaginable when he climbed in with the pigs and ate the food they were eating. No one should have ever spoken to him again for doing this.

Prayer

Before class cut out a large heart. Ask a child to say a number between one and the number of children in your class. Everyone count while passing the heart that number of times. The person holding the heart when it stops says the name of one person who loves him or her. Repeat, asking another child for a number, then counting and passing the heart again. Once everyone has had a turn, say this prayer together: **Dear God, thank you for loving us. And thank you for the people who love us. In Jesus' name, amen.**

Cleanup

Before class, cut a couple of very large hearts out of craft foam. To clean up at the end of your class, have two children hold the edges of one heart. Have another child place the items to be picked up onto the heart. Have them carry the heart full of toys to their final destinations. Have the children switch roles.

Homeward Bound

As the children leave, make sure they have their completed *Hold'em-Ups* they made for Bible Story Time. Encourage them to help tell the story of the father who loved and forgave his son. Fold red paper, then cut small two-layer hearts, keeping part of the fold on one side of each heart. Say, **See this heart,** then gently pinch the sides so the heart puffs out. **It is full of love, just like God's heart is full of love for you.**

* **Whose heart is full of love for you?**
* **Name three people who love you.**

Home Connections

It's a Snap!

In the Bible story of the Prodigal Son, the father never stopped loving his son, even when he did selfish things and made hurtful choices. God is like the father in the story. We might make bad choices that are very hurtful to others, ourselves and to God. But God loves us and forgives us despite what we do. Help your child understand the truly unconditional love that God has for everyone.

Home Connection

These are items that were used during the Bible story lesson that might be commonly found in your home. When your child sees or plays with one of the items mentioned below, help make the connection to the Bible story.

Suitcase: A suitcase was used in the lesson to demonstrate how the son packed up everything and left his father. But the father still loved his son no matter what he did. When your child sees a suitcase, remind him or her of the Prodigal Son Bible story. You can tell your child that God's heart is full of love for us, like a suitcase might be full of clothes.

Heart: There are typically many items in a home that might have a heart on them. When you see a heart, especially at Valentine's Day, talk about how people use a heart to express love. Talk about how God and people can have hearts full of love.

Keeping Connected

Here are two simple activities that were used in class during the Bible story lesson of God Is Full of Love. Use these activities to help your child remember the Bible story lesson.

A Little Taste of Love
Use a cookie cutter to cut out heart shapes from bread. Talk about how hearts remind you of love. Spread a little "love" on their bread hearts. Help your child spread jelly onto them. Talk about how God wants to spread his love to everyone.

God Loves Us (*Song/Finger Play*)
Sing to the tune of "Three Blind Mice."

> *God loves us; God loves us.*
> *Great is his love; great is his love.*
> *He loves us more than we can know.*
> *He loves us from our heads to our toes.*
> *God loves us; God loves us.*

Title: God Is Full of Love (Valentine's Day)

Bible Story: Prodigal Son
Luke 15:11–32

Bible Truth: God loves and forgives us. God loves everyone.

Bible Verse: Great is his love for us. (Psalm 117:2a)

- In this lesson, your child **heard** how a father loved and forgave his son, who had made bad choices.

- In this lesson, your child **learned** that like the father, God loves and forgives us, no matter what choices we make.

- In this lesson, your child **remembered** God has a great amount of love for us.

A Thankful Heart

(Thanksgiving)

BIBLE STORY:

Ten Lepers
Luke 17:11–19

BIBLE TRUTH:

I can be thankful for what God has done for me.

BIBLE VERSE:

Give thanks to the LORD, because he is good. (Psalm 136:1a)

Learning to be thankful is not only foundational to spiritual development, but it is also an essential life skill. As the children discover all of the wonderful things God has given to them and done for them, their hearts will spill over with thanks.

* In this lesson, children will **hear** the story of the 10 lepers who were healed and how only one returned with a thankful heart.

* In this lesson, children will **learn** that they can give thanks for the things God has done for them.

* In this lesson, children will **remember** to give thanks to God because he is so good to them.

Lesson Nine Snapshot

Get List:

- ☐ 1 copy of the *Hold'em-Up* reproducible (page 74) per child
- ☐ Scissors
- ☐ Crayons or markers
- ☐ Several buckets
- ☐ Paper
- ☐ Optional: Bucket of Thanks from Bible Story Link
- ☐ Rolls of bathroom tissue
- ☐ Stick-on bandages
- ☐ Health care items
- ☐ Stuffed animals or dolls
- ☐ 10 large polystyrene or plastic cups
- ☐ Horn-shaped snacks
- ☐ Fruit-flavored cereal balls
- ☐ 2 bowls
- ☐ Plates
- ☐ Bible
- ☐ 1 copy of *Home Connections* (page 79) for each child

The Heart of the Story:

The lepers asked for pity; Jesus gave them health plus restoration to their families and community. It was a significant gift of God's love and grace given through his power.

Jesus told them to go, and they did. If we give them the benefit of the doubt, that they went in faithful obedience knowing God was healing them, why didn't they immediately thank Jesus before going? It's a question we probably can't answer this side of eternity, but we can learn that it is better to thank God for his goodness somewhat late than not at all.

Be alert to readily thank Jesus for all his goodness yet to come and already given. Be forward-thinking and generous with gratitude. Encourage the children you teach to do the same.

Hold'em-Up
Bible Story Reproducible Page

- A copy of the reproducible on this page for each child
- Scissors
- Crayons or markers

Reproduce and cut out the figure for each child. Have the children color in the pictures, and then draw a picture of themselves in the small heart. Gently fold the heart on the broken line so the halves remain open. Have the children hold the hearts at the fold and use as talking puppet hearts.

I can be thankful for what God has done for me.

Give thanks to the LORD, because he is good. (Psalm 136:1a)

Give thanks to the LORD, because he is good. (Psalm 136:1a)

Round'em-Up

Use the *Round'em-Up* activities to gather the children or anytime you need a quick group activity for a transition or filler.

Bible Story Link

* Bucket
* Paper
* Scissors
* Marker

Bucket of Thanks

Before class cut out several hearts. In class, gather the children, and have the bucket and the hearts within your reach. Tell the children about several things you are thankful for. Then pull out the bucket and the hearts. Ask the children what they are thankful for and write their responses on the hearts. Put the hearts in the bucket. Tell the children this is your Bucket of Thanks. In the Bible story today, they'll learn about a man whose bucket was full of thanks.

Song/ Fingerplay

* Optional: Bucket of Thanks from Bible Story Link

I'm Thankful For ...

Ask the children to name one thing they are thankful for and suggest an action that resembles that item. For example, stars in the sky as you open and close your hands. Have the children say with you, **I'm thankful for stars in the sky,** as you open and close your hands like twinkling stars. Repeat for another thing a child is thankful for. You might use your Bucket of Thanks from the Bible Story Link for ideas.

Game

* Rolls of bathroom tissue

Wrap Up Wound

Tell the children that in the Bible story today, they will learn about some people who were very sick. They had to wear lots of bandages because their skin was sick. Show the children the bathroom tissue. Have the children wrap you up using the bathroom tissue. If you have other brave volunteers, you could make this a contest to see which group of children can wrap the adult up the fastest.

Show Me

* Stick-On Bandages

Bandage Stick'ems

Hand each child a stick-on bandage. Have them pretend to stick them onto different body parts. Have the children show you how they can put one on their knee, elbow, tummy, shoulder or head. Talk about times when they were sick or needed a bandage.

Bible Story
Hands-on Activities

These activities work well for large or small groups of children, or as stations, to introduce and/or reinforce the Bible story.

Healing the Sick

* Bandages
* Health care items
* Stuffed animals or dolls

Provide the children with items to help others who might be sick. You might provide stuffed animals or dolls for the children. Talk with your class about times when they were sick. Tell them that in the Bible story, they will learn about some men who were very sick.

The Thankful One

* 10 large polystyrene or plastic cups

Show how to build a pyramid with four cups on the bottom row, then three cups, then two cups and finally one cup on the top. When placing the top cup, everyone shouts, "One thankful heart!" Tell them that in the Bible story they will learn how Jesus healed 10 men, but only one thanked Jesus for what he had done.

Bible Memory

* Paper
* Scissors

Give thanks to the Lord, because he is good. (Psalm 136:1a)

Cut one heart from paper for every two children. Have the children sit on the floor in pairs facing their partners with their legs slightly spread in a V and touching feet to feet. Hand one person in each pair a heart. That partner says, "Give thanks to the Lord," while reaching to pass the heart. The other partner takes the heart, and hands it back while saying, "because he is good." Have each pair pass their heart back and forth, each child saying their part of the Bible verse at each pass. See how quickly each pair of children can pass their hearts but still say the verse together. Change partners.

Cornucopia of Thanks

* Horn-shaped snacks
* Fruit-flavored cereal balls
* 2 bowls
* Plates

Pour the horn-shaped snacks and fruit-flavored cereal balls into separate bowls. Hand out plates to each child. Show the children the horn-shaped snacks and tell them these are little baskets called cornucopias. (Or you might call them "buckets.") Have the children use the baskets to scoop up cereal, then put each filled basket on their plates. Have children name things they are thankful for. *Note: Check with parents for any food allergies children may have.*

Bible Story Time

- Bible
- Completed *Hold'em-Up* (from page 74) for each child

Gather your children for Story Time; be sure all the children have their *Hold'em-Ups* ready to go. Show the children how to use their talking hearts like puppet mouths as they repeat, "Thank you, thank you, thank you, Jesus. Thank you, thank you, from my heart." Let them know they'll say other things too, as you tell this Bible story.

Hold up a Bible for the children to see. **Our Bible story is found in the book of Luke. It tells us a story about 10 men who were very sick. The men had a very bad skin disease that would never heal. They were so sick they could not be around other people. They could not be with their families.**

One important part we will learn is most of the men did not have thankful hearts. Have the children show closed puppet hearts.

One day Jesus walked by the 10 men and they went up to Jesus, but they still stayed away so they wouldn't make others sick. The 10 men asked Jesus to help them. They knew that Jesus could heal people and make them well again. Have the children open and close their hearts while saying, "Oooh" and "aah."

Jesus told the 10 men to go home, and they went. On the way, they started screaming and shouting because they discovered they were healed. Have the children open and close their puppets as if screaming and shouting.

One of the 10 men turned around and went back to thank Jesus for healing him. He said …. Have the children repeat the phrase they practiced.

That's right. The man was very thankful and told Jesus …. Have the children repeat the phrase again.

We can tell Jesus we are thankful for what he does for us too. God is good to us. Let's use our hearts to tell him how thankful we are. Have the children repeat the phrase.

- **Who healed the 10 men?** *(Jesus)*
- **How can we thank Jesus?** *(prayer, music, worship, and so on)*
- **What has Jesus done that we can thank him for?**

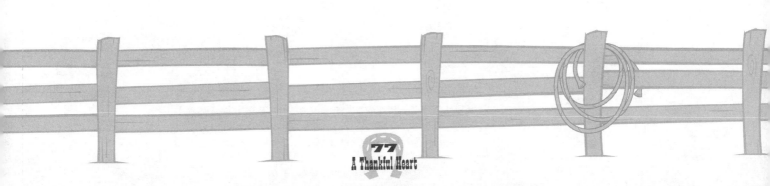

Send'em-Off

- ★ Bucket of Thanks from Bible Story Link
- ★ Buckets
- ★ Completed *Hold'em-Up* for each child
- ★ Bathroom tissue

Prayer

Gather the children in a circle and pass your Bucket of Thanks from the Bible Story Link in *Round'em-Up* around. As you pass the bucket say, **Thank you Lord, for giving us the things we need for living.** Whoever receives the bucket on *living*, pull out a heart. Read the item written on the heart. Then pass the bucket again and repeat until everyone has had a turn.

Cleanup

Give all the children or pairs buckets for cleanup. Have the children gather toys and items to put away. Tell the children that the buckets remind you of having a bucket full of thanks. Have the children talk about what they are thankful for as they fill their buckets and place the items back where they belong.

Homeward Bound

As the children leave, make sure they have their completed *Hold'em-Ups* they made for Bible Story Time. Tie a little bit of bathroom tissue around their wrists as they leave to remind them of the man in the Bible story who had a thankful heart.

★ **What are you thankful for?**

Teacher Tip

One child keeps trying to use his heart to nip or bite at other children. Ask him to show how to use his heart the right way. If he continues, tell him that he can use the heart the right way or it will have to be put on the table for awhile. Allow him to choose. If he doesn't choose, then you choose for him.

Itty Bitty Bible Facts

Leprosy was a chronic disease that led to paralysis, wasting of muscle, deformities and mutilations. These men were separated from their families and friends as "unclean," yet Jesus approached them, loved them and healed them.

Home Connections

It's a Snap!

Title: A Thankful Heart (Thanksgiving)

Bible Story: Ten Lepers *Luke 17:11–19*

Bible Truth: I can be thankful for what God has done for me.

Bible Verse: Give thanks to the LORD because he is good. (Psalm 136:1a)

- In this lesson, your child **heard** the story of the 10 lepers who were healed and how only one returned with a thankful heart.

- In this lesson, your child **learned** to give thanks for the things that God has done.

- In this lesson, your child **remembered** to give thanks to God because he is good.

In this Bible story, each one of the 10 sick men was special to Jesus. When Jesus saw the men who needed his healing, he did not turn away from them. He cared about them and healed them. God did an incredible thing for the men on that day, but only one man returned to thank Jesus. Teach your little one to have a thankful heart for all that Jesus does for us.

Home Connection

These are items that were used during the Bible story lesson that might be commonly found in your home. When your child sees or plays with one of the items mentioned below, help make the connection to the Bible story.

Bucket: A bucket was used to show how the children can have a Bucket of Thanks for all that Jesus does for them. On some paper hearts, write some things that you as a family are thankful for. Then put them in your own Bucket of Thanks.

Bathroom Tissue: Bathroom tissue was used as bandages. The Bible story was about men who had leprosy, a terrible disease. Bandages were used to care for the wounds of those who had leprosy. Talk about how Jesus healed the lepers.

Keeping Connected

Here are two simple activities that were used in class during the Bible story lesson of A Thankful Heart. Use these activities to help your child remember the Bible story lesson.

The Thankful One

Show your child how to turn plastic cups upside down and build a pyramid. You will need 10 cups all together. There will be four cups on the bottom row, then three cups, then two cups and finally one cup on the top. When the top cup is placed shout, "One thankful heart!" Talk about how in the Bible story 10 men were healed, but only one of the men came back to thank Jesus for what he did. Encourage your child to have a thankful heart like the one man.

I'm Thankful for ... *(Song/Fingerplay)*

Name something you're thankful for and create an action that resembles that item. For example, stars in the sky as you open and close your hands. Say together, **I'm thankful for stars in the sky,** as you open and close your hands like twinkling stars. Repeat for other things or pull hearts from your Bucket of Thanks and create fingerplays for those ideas.

Jesus and the Little Guy

BIBLE STORY:
Zacchaeus
Luke 19:1–10

BIBLE TRUTH:
God loves us;
we can love others.

BIBLE VERSE:
We love because
he loved us first.
(1 John 4:19)

It's very easy to love those who love us. But what about the people who do things that hurt us or make it hard to love them? Young children have a natural tendency to be very accepting of most people. Encourage them to show their love toward others, especially those who might be hard to love.

* In this lesson, children will **hear** how Jesus showed his love to a man who was not very nice.

* In this lesson, children will **learn** that God loves us deeply. Because God loves us, we can show our love to others.

* In this lesson, children will **remember** that we can love others because God loved us first.

Lesson Ten Snapshot

Get List:

- [ ] 1 copy of the *Hold'em-Up* reproducible (page 82) per child
- [ ] Scissors
- [ ] Hole Punch
- [ ] Crayons and markers
- [ ] Paper fastener
- [ ] 20 index cards
- [ ] Poster board
- [ ] Craft sticks
- [ ] Leaves
- [ ] Copy paper
- [ ] Optional: Pencils
- [ ] Masking tape
- [ ] Assorted lettuce leaves
- [ ] Broccoli flowerets
- [ ] Celery sticks
- [ ] Ranch dip
- [ ] Bible
- [ ] Small tree branch
- [ ] 1 copy of *Home Connections* (page 87) for each child

The Heart of the Story:

Love is not only the heart of this story, it makes the story. People ostracized Zacchaeus, possibly in the hope such action would cause Zacchaeus to change. That obviously didn't work, but love did. Love not only changed Zacchaeus, it prompted him to strive to reverse some of the harm he had caused.

We might have a lot of different thoughts and emotions for people. We know we should let love rise to the top and shine, but that isn't always our experience. Other stuff slips out. It is as if Jesus says through this story, "I love you. Receive my love and let it fill you. Then you'll be amazed at how easily you love others, because my love is in you." Let God love you, then let his love flow through.

Hold'em-Up
Bible Story Reproducible Page

- 1 copy of the reprodicible on this page for each child
- Scissors
- Hole punch
- Crayons or markers
- Paper fastener

Copy and cut out the tree figure and circle for each child. Punch the center holes. Children color the pictures and draw themselves in the blank section of the circle. Put the tree over the circle and insert the paper fastener through the center holes. Spread the brad. Show the children how the circle turns and and the pictures show in the opening.

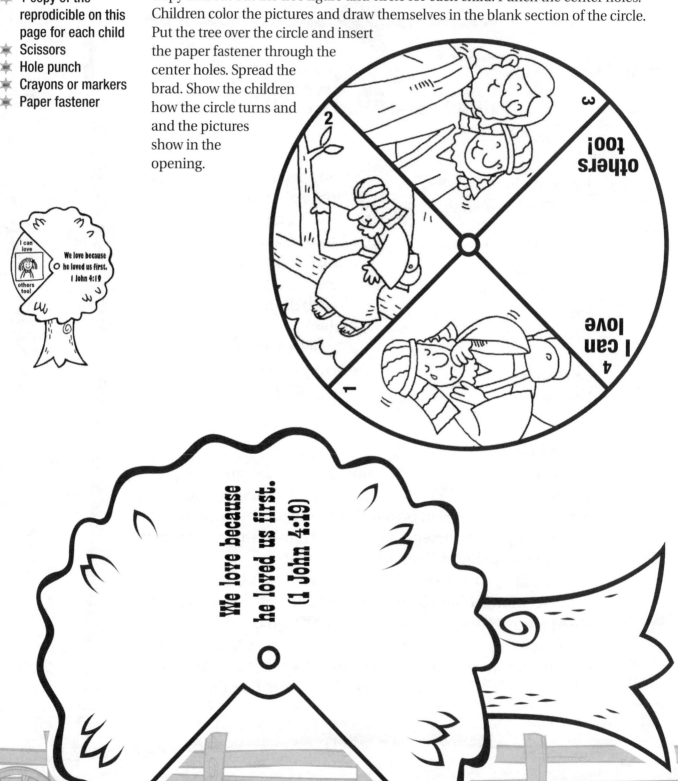

I can love others too!

We love because he loved us first. 1 John 4:19

We love because he loved us first. (1 John 4:19)

Round'em-Up

Use the *Round'em-Up* activities to gather the children or anytime you need a quick group activity for a transition or filler.

Bible Story Link

* 20 index cards
* Markers
* Scissors

Flip a Smile

Before class, cut 20 circles from the index cards. On one side, draw a smiley face; on the other side, draw a sad face. In class, gather the children and show them both sides of a face. Talk about things that make us happy and things that make us sad. Spread the faces on the floor with the sad side up. Tell the children Jesus can turn our sad faces into happy faces. Have the children turn the faces over as fast as they can. Collect the faces and repeat.

Game

* Poster board
* Scissors
* Marker

Happy Face, Sad Face

Cut a very large circle from poster board. On one side, draw a happy face; on the other side, draw a sad face. Have all the children stand at one side of the room. When you show the happy face, they can crawl toward you. When you show the sad face, they must freeze. The goal is to have all the children reach your happy face. Talk about how everyone needs a friend.

Song/ Fingerplay

Zacchaeus Was a Tiny Man

Read this poem aloud as you lead the children in the actions.

Zacchaeus was a tiny man; he was a thief and bad.
(crouch down and get small)
Nobody liked him; his heart was very sad.
(show sad faces)
He climbed into a great big tree to see what he could see. (pretend to climb and look around)
And soon he saw Jesus, walking by the tree.
(point up into a tree)
Jesus saw Zacchaeus and it turned his heart around. (turn around)
We can be like Jesus and love others too.
(wrap arms around self)
We can be the best of friends, me and you.
(find a friend and put arms around each other's shoulder, or point to friend)

Show Me

Trees in the Breeze

Have the children spread out so they have room to move. Ask them to stand tall and spreading their arms as if they are trees along the road Jesus walked. Then have them sway and move their arms like a tree in a very strong breeze. Ask them to think about how a tree might feel, if it could, when someone is climbing it. Let them show you how a tree might act when climbed. Tell the children your Bible story is about a man who climbed a tree to see Jesus.

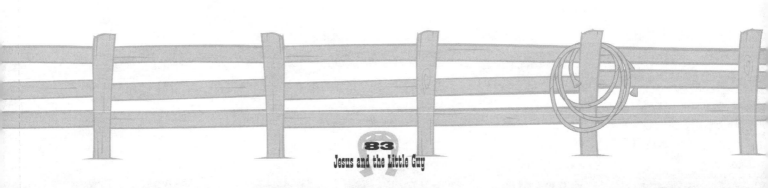

Bible Story
Hands-on Activities

These activities work well for large or small groups of children, or as stations, to introduce and/or reinforce the Bible story.

Activity 1

★ Craft sticks

Friendship Trees

Give the children a handful of craft sticks. Have them lay the sticks out to make a tree. Then have them clear off their work area and start again but add more craft sticks for them to use. Talk about how Zacchaeus needed a friend, so he climbed a tree to see Jesus.

Activity 3

★ Masking tape

Bible Memory

We love because he loved us first. (1 John 4:19)

Put masking tape on the floor to make a tree trunk. Add eight branches, spaced in large steps up the tree. Have the children line up at the base of the tree, say the first word of the verse and jump to the first branch. Continue through the verse and reference while jumping from branch to branch climbing up the tree. Turn around to repeat working your way back down.

Activity 2

★ Crayons
★ Leaves
★ Copy paper
★ Optional: Pencils

Rubbing Off Friendship

Before class, peel wrappers off the crayons and gather various sizes and shapes of leaves. In class, place a leaf on the table. Show the children how to put a piece of paper over the leaf. Then gently color over the paper with the side of a crayon or pencil. Tell the children that Zacchaeus needed a friend, so he climbed a tree. Talk about people they know who need a friend. You can write these names on the pictures.

Activity 4

★ Assorted lettuce leaves
★ Broccoli flowerets
★ Celery sticks
★ Ranch dip

Friendly Trees

Provide assorted lettuce leaves, celery sticks and broccoli flowerets. Talk about how all of these things remind you of trees. Tell them how Zacchaeus climbed a tree to see Jesus because he needed a friend. Provide ranch dip. As the children eat their snack, have them talk about their friends. Then talk about how they can be a friend to others. Ask them if they know what friends do to show kindness to each other. *Note: Check with parents for any food allergies children may have.*

Bible Story Time

- Bible
- Completed *Hold'em-Up* (from page 82) for each child

Gather your children for Story Time; be sure all the children have their *Hold'em-Ups* ready to go. Hold up a Bible for the children to see.

In the Bible, we read a story about a man who was sad because he did not have many friends. Have the children turn to picture #1. **This is the man without enough friends. His name was Zacchaeus.** Have the children repeat the name with you. **Zacchaeus didn't have many friends because he was not very nice to people.**

One day, Jesus came to the town where Zaccheus lived. Everyone wanted to see Jesus, including Zacchaeus. Zacchaeus was afraid that he was not going to be able to see Jesus when he walked by because Zacchaeus was short. The people who didn't like Zacchaeus wouldn't let him stand in front of them, even though they could easily see over Zacchaeus and still see Jesus.

Have the children turn to picture #2. **This shows what Zacchaeus did. He climbed into a tree so he could see Jesus.**

Have the children turn to picture #3. **This is Jesus and Zacchaeus. Zacchaeus learned that Jesus was his friend. Since Jesus loved Zacchaeus, Zaccheus decided he could be nice to people. Because of Jesus, Zacchaeus changed. Now people liked Zacchaeus.**

Have the children turn to picture #4. **Who is in your pictures?** *(I am, each of us, we are)* **Each of us can be friends with others, just like Jesus was friends with Zacchaeus. We can show others Jesus' love and be friends with them. Because Jesus loves each of us, we can love others too.**

- **Who loved Zaccheus?** *(Jesus)*
- **Who wants us to love others and be friends?** *(Jesus)*
- **What can you do to show others you love them?**

Send'em-Off

- Small tree branch
- Leaves
- Completed *Hold'em-Up* for each child

Prayer

Have the children join you in a circle on the floor. Pass a small tree branch around and have each child holding the branch say the name of a friend. Have each child pray: **Dear God, thank you for my friend, (name). Help me to be kind and show** (him/her) **love. In Jesus' name, amen.**

Teacher Tip

Make a leaf collection using different types of leaves. Then talk about how friends are different, just like all of the different leaves. Talk about the different qualities friends have.

Cleanup

Tell the children that during cleanup time you will say, **Show me your friendship tree.** That's when they stop and put their arms out as if they are a tree. They stay until you come by to touch each one to unfreeze them. When you touch them say, **(child's name) is a good friend.** Begin cleanup and repeat as often as you wish.

Homeward Bound

As the children leave, make sure they have their completed *Hold'em-Ups* they made for Bible Story Time. Hand the children a leaf as they exit your class. Tell them the leaf reminds you of the tree Zacchaeus climbed so that he could see Jesus. Jesus was a good friend to Zacchaeus, and you can be a good friend too.

Itty Bitty Bible Facts

The tree that Zacchaeus climbed was a sycamore tree. It has large strong branches that make it perfect for climbing.

- **Tell me the names of two of your friends.**
- **What does your leaf remind you of?**

Home Connections

It's a Snap!

Title: Jesus and the Little Guy

Bible Story: Zacchaeus *Luke 19:1–10*

Bible Truth: God loves us; we can love others.

Bible Verse: We love because he loved us first. (1 John 4:19)

- In this lesson, your child **heard** how Jesus showed his love to a man who was not very nice.

- In this lesson, your child **learned** that God loves us deeply. Because God loves us, we can show our love to others.

- In this lesson, your child **remembered** that we can love others because God loved us first.

Zacchaeus was well-known, but for the wrong reasons. He also received a lot of attention, but the wrong kind. Jesus viewed Zacchaeus with love. Apparently, no one else did that. But it was love that prompted Zacchaeus to change. God's love, demonstrted by Jesus, made the difference. Because God loves us, we can love others. The important first step is understanding and accepting God's love for each of us. Childhood is the best time to begin. Help your child make that first step and keep walking in God's love.

Home Connection

These are items that were used during the Bible story lesson that might be commonly found in your home. When your child sees or plays with one of the items mentioned below, help make the connection to the Bible story.

Trees and Leaves: Several activities involved trees and leaves. Go for a walk and collect different shapes and sizes of leaves. As you walk, talk about how trees remind you of the Bible story of Zacchaeus. Tell your child Jesus loved Zacchaeus and Jesus loves each of us too. Since God loves us we can love others.

Smiley Face: When you see a smiley face, you can remind your child of the Bible story. Talk about things that make you happy and things that make you sad. Jesus wants us to love one another; it makes him happy.

Keeping Connected

Here are two simple activities that were used in class during the Bible story lesson of Jesus and the Little Guy. Use these activities to help your child remember the Bible story lesson.

Bible Memory

We love because he loved us first. (1 John 4:19)
Use sidewalk chalk to draw a tree with eight branches placed so your child can jump from one to another. Starting at the base of the tree, say the first word of the Bible Verse together, then hold hands and jump to the first branch. Say the second word and jump to the next branch. Continue jumping to branches saying the verse and reference. Then climb down.

Friendship Trees

Put out a handful of craft sticks for you and your child to make a tree as big as you can. Then bring out more craft sticks to make your tree even bigger. Talk about how Zacchaeus climbed a big tree to see Jesus.

The Super Duper Supper

BIBLE STORY:

Jesus Feeds 5,000
John 6:1–14

BIBLE TRUTH:

God wants us to help others.

BIBLE VERSE:

We will serve the LORD.
(Joshua 24:15b)

Young children are little, but they can be a big help. This story is about a small boy who was a big help by giving everything he had to Jesus. In turn, Jesus performed a miracle. Let your children know that although they are little, they can be super duper helpers.

⭐ In this lesson, children will **hear** the story of the boy who helped Jesus by giving him his supper. Jesus used the little supper to perform a great big miracle.

⭐ In this lesson, children will **learn** that no matter what our size or age, God wants us to help others.

⭐ In this lesson, children will **remember** to be helpful and serve the Lord.

Lesson Eleven Snapshot

Get List:

- ☐ 1 copy of the *Hold'em-Up* reproducible (page 90) for each child
- ☐ Small brown paper lunch sacks
- ☐ Scissors
- ☐ Crayons and markers
- ☐ Index cards
- ☐ Serving tray
- ☐ Bag of cotton balls
- ☐ Place mats
- ☐ Plastic dinnerware and food

- ☐ 2 cups flour
- ☐ 1 cup salt
- ☐ 1 cup water
- ☐ Vegetable oil
- ☐ Paper plates
- ☐ Bible
- ☐ Pitas
- ☐ Fish-shaped crackers
- ☐ CD player and music CD
- ☐ Variety of baskets
- ☐ 1 copy of *Home Connections* (page 95) for each child

The Heart of the Story:

Jesus saw the crowd and knew everyone in it. He knew they were hungry for dinner and miracles of healing and salvation. Jesus saw the boy as well, and recognized the boy's desire to help others and willingness to play a part in the plan Jesus had in mind. The boy's desire, his simple help and God's divine intervention met the physical needs of thousands. Now, we are too late to join in the dinner, but we do get a lesson in what matters when it comes to helping.

God is more interested in our desire and initiative to help than in how much we have to offer or even how much we actually give. That's because God's specialty is miracles. He loves doing the miraculous, like making a simple supper super. Our part is simply a willingness to help and the humility to go along with Jesus for his plan.

Hold'em-Up
Bible Story Reproducible Page

* 1 copy of the reproducible on this page for each child
* Brown paper lunch sacks
* Scissors
* Crayons or markers

Copy and cut out the loaves and the fish figures for each child. Have the children color the pictures. Show them how to accordion fold the loaves then unfold, one at a time, counting up to five. The fish also fold to show one fish, then two fish. Put the fish and loaves in lunch sacks. Label the lunch sacks with the children's names.

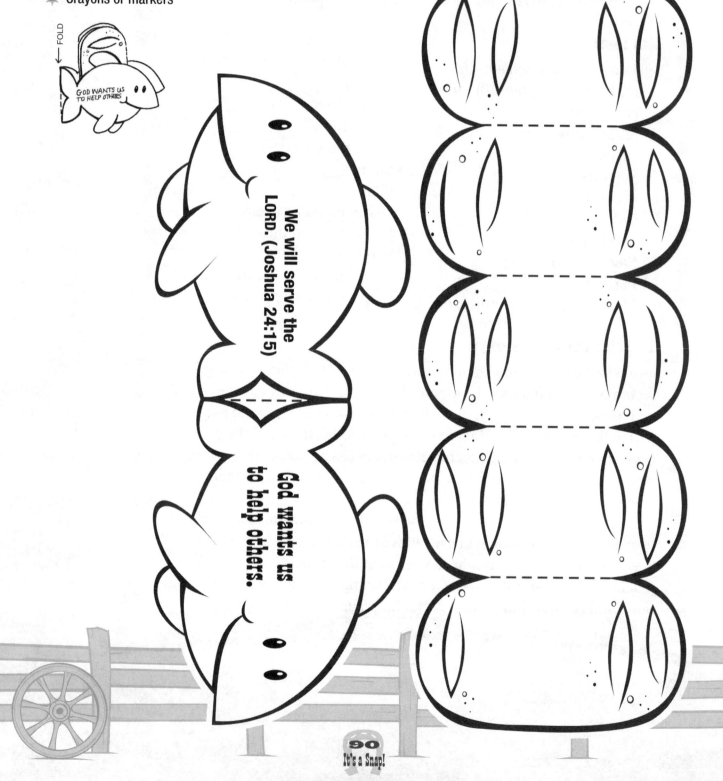

We will serve the LORD. (Joshua 24:15)

God wants us to help others.

GOD WANTS US TO HELP OTHERS

FOLD

Round'em-Up

Use the *Round'em-Up* activities to gather the children or anytime you need a quick group activity for a transition or filler.

Serve Others

* Index cards
* Scissors
* Markers
* Serving tray

Before class, cut out fish and bread shapes from the index cards. See the suggested shapes below. In class, gather the children and talk about ways that they can help or serve others around home, at church or with friends. Write each response on an index card and place it on a serving tray. Talk about how we can help others by doing kind things for them. Then drop the cards on the floor. Shout, **Let's serve others,** and have the children pick up the cards and put them on the tray again.

One Bun, Two …

Chant to the rhythm of "One Potato, Two Potato."

One bun (lift one finger),
two buns (lift two fingers),
three buns (lift three fingers),
four (lift four fingers),
five little buns I give to the Lord (lift five fingers).
One fish (lift one finger),
two fish (lift two fingers),
that's all—(lift both hands),
pray (fold hands in prayer)*!*
God will meet my needs today.

Pick Up the Leftovers

* Small paper lunch sacks
* Bag of cotton balls
* Marker

Before class, use a marker to mark 5 to 10 cotton balls and return them to your bag of cotton balls. In class, tell the children that in the Bible story a little boy helped Jesus when he shared his supper. Jesus then used his supper to feed 5,000 people. There was so much food that there were leftovers.

Hand each child a paper lunch sack. Spread all your cotton balls (marked ones as fish and unmarked as bread) on the floor. Have the children help you pick up the leftovers. See which child has the most marked cotton balls (fish), and then he or she can help spread out the cotton balls for the next game.

A Fishy Tail

Have the children show you how they can swim like fish. Have them swim fast and slow. Have them show you how a big fish would swim and how a little fish would swim. Have them show you what a fish in a lunch sack would look like. Talk about how the boy had two fish in his supper. Then have the children swim to find a fish partner.

Bible Story
Hands-on Activities

These activities work well for large or small groups of children, or as stations, to introduce and/or reinforce the Bible story.

Activity 1

* Place mats
* Plastic dinnerware and food

Super Duper Supper

Provide place mats, plastic dinnerware and plastic food for the children to use in pretending to be at a feast. Talk about how the boy helped Jesus by giving him his supper. Jesus then used the boy's food to make a giant feast for lots of people. Talk about ways they can be helpful to others.

Activity 2

* 2 cups flour
* 1 cup salt
* 1 cup water
* Vegetable oil
* Paper plates

Loaves and Fishes

Before class, make play dough by mixing 1 cup salt, 2 cups flour, 1 cup water and 1 Tbsp. oil. Talk about how the boy was helpful to Jesus by giving him his supper of five loaves of bread and two fish. Give each child a clump of dough and a paper plate. Have the children make loaves and fish using the dough. Talk about ways they can help others.

Activity 3

* Bible

Bible Memory

We will serve the LORD. (Joshua 24:15)

Show the children a Bible. Tell them the Bible says to serve the Lord, just like the little boy in the Bible story served the Lord by giving Jesus his supper. Have each child find a partner. Have them repeat the words and actions after you. **We will** (have the children point to each other) **serve the** (have the children slap hands with their partners with each word) **Lord** (have the children point up). Repeat several times and then switch partners.

Activity 4

* Pitas
* Fish-shaped crackers

Super Supper

Before class, cut the pitas so each child can have one half. In class, hand each child a pita half. Tell them this is like the bread the boy had in his supper. Then tell them the boy also had some fish in his supper, and hand out the fish crackers. The children can put their fish into their pitas. Explain how helpful the boy was to Jesus. Talk about ways they can be helpful too. *Note: Check with parents for any food allergies children may have.*

Bible Story Time

* Bible
* Completed *Hold'em-Up* (from page 96) for each child
* Small paper lunch sacks

Teacher Tip

Here's a simple modification to help meet the special needs of children who have difficulty with fine motor skills such as reaching into a bag or folding and unfolding the loaves and fish. Unfold the loaves and fish, then staple them to the outside of a lunch sack. Have the children hold up their sacks at the appropriate time in your Bible story.

Gather your children for Story Time; be sure all the children have their *Hold'em-Ups* ready to go. Hold up a Bible for the children to see.

In the Bible, there is a story about a boy who was very helpful to Jesus. One day a boy went on a hike to a place called the Sea of Galilee. The boy carried with him a bag that had his supper in it. You have a bag similar to what the boy had. Let's see what's in your bag.

Have the children pull out the loaves and the fish as you say this rhyme:

> *The boy had one bun, two buns, three buns, four,*
> *five little buns, but there were more.*
> *The boy had one fish, two fish, and that is all the fish.*
> *The boy helped Jesus as he wished.*

Have the children put their items back into their bags. **The boy traveled with a very, very large group of people who were following Jesus. Not just five people, not just 10 people, but more than 100 people. The people began to get hungry, so the little boy wanted to help. The little boy wanted to give his supper to Jesus. But his supper was only …** have the children pull out their loaves and fish as you repeat the rhyme.

That was not enough to feed all the people. But Jesus knew it was enough. Jesus took the little supper from the boy. He took … have the children pull out their loaves and fish as you repeat the rhyme.

Then Jesus prayed over the little supper. The little boy helped Jesus serve the food. Soon there was more food than what the people could eat. There were even leftovers. Even though the boy was small, he was very helpful. Jesus could turn his little supper into a great, big, huge, super duper, supper.

* **Who helped Jesus by giving his supper to him?** *(the boy with five loaves and two fish)*
* **Who can be helpful like the boy in the Bible story?** *(each of us)*
* **Who can serve the Lord?** *(we can)*

Send'em-Off

- CD player and music CD
- Serving tray
- Variety of baskets
- Completed *Hold'em-Up* for each child

Prayer

Have the children sit in a circle. Play your music CD and have the children pass the serving tray around. Stop the music and ask the child holding the tray to tell who he or she would like to help or serve. Start the music and repeat until each child has had a turn. Then lead the children in this prayer: **Dear God, bless the people that we know. Let us help them as we grow. In Jesus' name, amen.**

Cleanup

Tell the children that because the boy was helpful, Jesus prayed and made lots of food. They collected the extra food, or leftovers, in baskets. Have the children collect their "leftovers" in baskets too.

Homeward Bound

As the children leave, make sure they have their completed *Hold'em-Ups* they made for Bible Story Time. Have them say the Bible Verse with you and perform the motions that go with it. "We will serve the LORD" (Joshua 24:15b).

- **What is one way you can be helpful to the Lord?**
- **Who wants you to be helpful?**

Itty Bitty Bible Facts

The boy in the story was very young–perhaps around the age of five. The type of grain used for the bread was barley. This was grain used by poor people. The boy was poor, but still wanted to help by sharing what he had.

Home Connections

It's a Snap!

The little boy in this story was very helpful by giving his supper to Jesus. Then Jesus did a miracle and made a super duper supper for more than 5,000 people! Even though Jesus did most of the work, the boy had a special part in helping. God wants us to help him do his work. Even though your child may be little, he or she can have a huge impact on helping others, especially helping Jesus.

Home Connection

These are items that were used during the Bible story lesson that might be commonly found in your home. When your child sees or plays with one of the items mentioned below, help make the connection to the Bible story.

Bread: The boy had five small loaves of bread in his supper. Whenever you have some bread, remind your child about the boy who was helpful to Jesus and others because he shared his bread. Talk about ways that your child can share and be helpful to others.

Brown paper lunch sack: Lunch sacks were used to help tell the Bible story. Whenever you use a lunch sack, remind your child about the supper the boy shared with Jesus. Talk about ways that your child can share and help others.

Keeping Connected

Here are two simple activities that were used in class during the Bible story lesson of The Super Duper Supper. Use these activities to help your child remember that God wants us to help others.

Loaves and Fishes

Make play dough by mixing 1 cup salt, 2 cups flour, 1 cup water and 1 Tbsp. vegetable oil. Talk about how the boy was helpful to Jesus by giving him his supper of five loaves of bread and two fish. Give your child a clump of dough and a paper plate. Have your child make loaves of bread and fish using the dough. Talk about ways they can share and help others.

One Bun, Two ... *(Song/Finger Play)*

Chant to the rhythm of "One Potato, Two Potato."

One bun (lift one finger), *two buns* (lift two fingers),
three buns (lift three fingers), *four* (lift four fingers),
five little buns I give to the Lord (lift five fingers).
One fish (lift one finger), *two fish* (lift two fingers),
that's all—(lift both hands), *pray* (fold hands in prayer)*!*
God will meet my needs today.

Title: The Super Duper Supper

Bible Story: Jesus Feeds 5,000 *John 6:1–14*

Bible Truth: God wants us to help others.

Bible Verse: We will serve the LORD. (Joshua 24:15b)

- In this lesson, your child **heard** the story of the boy who helped Jesus by giving him his supper. Jesus used the little supper to perform a great big miracle.

- In this lesson, your child **learned** that no matter what our size or age, God wants us to help others.

- In this lesson, your child **remembered** to be helpful and serve the Lord.

The Good Shepherd

BIBLE STORY:

The Lost Sheep
Luke 15:1–7

BIBLE TRUTH:

You are precious
to God.

BIBLE VERSE:

He takes good care
of those who trust in
him. (Nahum 1:7b)

Children need to know how precious and valuable they are to God. Teach your little ones that they can always trust God to protect them, guide them and provide for them. He has given his life in exchange for theirs and he will search for them when they have gone astray. They are his little lambs and he truly is their Good Shepherd.

⭐ In this lesson, children will **hear** how the shepherd searched for his lost lamb because there is nothing more precious to a shepherd than his lambs.

⭐ In this lesson, children will **learn** that they are precious to God, just as a lamb is precious to a shepherd.

⭐ In this lesson, children will **remember** that God will take good care of those who put their trust in him. They can trust God because they are valuable to him.

Lesson Twelve Snapshot

Get List:

- ☐ 1 copy of the *Hold'em-Up* reproducible (page 98) for each child
- ☐ Scissors
- ☐ Cotton balls
- ☐ Glue
- ☐ Crayons and markers
- ☐ Paper
- ☐ Optional: toy lambs
- ☐ Several pairs of white socks
- ☐ Large empty box
- ☐ Masking tape
- ☐ Drinking straws
- ☐ Large and small marshmallows
- ☐ Pretzel sticks
- ☐ Paper plates
- ☐ Bible
- ☐ 1 copy of *Home Connections* (page 103) for each child

The Heart of the Story:

Every sheep matters enough that the shepherd pursues each one relentlessly, even taking personal risk, to assure all are safe and secure. This real-life example revealed God's heart for people long ago and for us today.

God pursues each of us to assure our safety and security. It leaves us overwhelmed. The Creator and sustainer of all knows each of us and regards us so highly that he goes after each one of us. The young children you teach will begin to understand how precious they are to God through the Bible story, your lesson and the way you interact with them and love them. You become a sort of shepherd simply by leading them to Jesus, who is also seeking each of them.

Hold'em-Up

Bible Story Reproducible Page

- 1 copy of the reproducible on this page for each child
- Scissors
- Cotton balls
- Glue
- Crayons or markers

Copy and cut out the sheep figure for each child. Cut out the two finger-holes as indicated. Have the children glue cotton balls on the head. Let the children color the sheep. Show the children how to put fingers through the holes to move the puppet.

He takes good care …

… of those who trust in him. (Nahum 1:7b)

You are precious to God.

CUT OUT   CUT OUT

Round'em-Up

Use the *Round'em-Up* activities to gather the children or anytime you need a quick group activity for a transition or filler.

Bible Story Link

* Paper
* Scissors
* Optional: toy lambs

Where Is the Lamb?

Before class, cut out three or four paper lambs or collect several soft toy lambs. Hide the lambs before children arrive. During class, gather the children and tell them that today they will learn about a shepherd who is looking for his lost sheep. Have the children look for the lost sheep in the room. If needed, help them with "hot" or "cold" clues as they move closer to or farther from the hidden lambs.

Song/ Fingerplay

You Are Precious

Sing this responsive song to the tune of "Where is Thumbkin?"

Verse 1
(Teacher) *You are precious, you are precious.*
(Children) *Yes, I am. Yes, I am.*
(Teacher) *You are very precious.*
You are very precious.
(Children) *Yes, I am. Yes, I am.*

Verse 2
(Teacher) *Where are the little lambs?*
Where are the little lambs?
(Children) *Here we are. Here we are.*
(Teacher) *Jesus loves my little lambs.*
Jesus loves my little lambs.
(Children) *Here we are. Here we are.*

Game

Good Shepherd Tag

Select one child to be a shepherd, another the wolf and the remainder sheep. The wolf is "It." The wolf's job will be to gently tag the sheep. When tagged, each sheep must freeze into a lamb chop. The good shepherd comes to the rescue by tagging the "frozen" lamb chops, turning them back into sheep. The sheep are then free to run and play again.

Show Me

Sheep

Have the children pretend to be sheep. They can pretend to eat and sleep. Have them show you how they can make themselves appear as large sheep or little sheep. Have them gather as a flock of sheep. Let the sheep run, jump and then hide as if lost in your room. Go find all your sheep and bring them around you.

Bible Story
Hands-on Activities

These activities work well for large or small groups of children, or as stations, to introduce and/or reinforce the Bible story.

Sock Sheep

* Several pairs of white socks
* Marker
* Large empty box

Before class, draw eyes, ears, nose and mouth on the toe-end of clean white socks. In class, show the children how to pull socks over their hands for puppet sheep. Use the cardboard from a large box as a pen for the sheep. Tell the children how shepherds love their sheep and care for them.

Bible Memory

He takes good care of those who trust in him. (Nahum 1:7b)

Teach the Bible Verse as a cheer by saying two words at a time for the children to echo back. Repeat using three or four words at a time. Be sure to include the reference. Then form two flocks with the children so one flock echoes back what the other flock says.

Sheep Pen

* Masking tape
* Cotton balls
* Drinking straws

Use masking tape to mark a square sheep pen in the center of a tabletop. Spread cotton balls on the table but outside the pen. Tell the children that the cotton balls represent sheep. Hand out straws to the children. Tell them to be good shepherds, and using their straws, blow the sheep into the pen. Explain that good shepherds take care of their sheep because they are so precious.

Little Lambs

* Large and small marshmallows
* Pretzel sticks
* Paper plates

Hand each child a paper plate. Put out pretzel sticks and marshmallows. Show the children how they can use the pretzels to connect marshmallows to make little lambs. They can also use the food items to build sheep pens. Talk about how shepherds take care of their little lambs. *Note: Check with parents for any food allergies children may have.*

Bible Story Time

- Bible
- Completed *Hold'em-Up* (from page 98) for each child

Gather your children for Story Time; be sure all the children have their *Hold'em-Ups* ready to go. Hold up a Bible for the children to see.

In the Bible, you will find a story about a sheep and a shepherd. Anytime you hear me say the word "sheep," I want you to hold up your little <u>sheep</u> and say, "Baa, baa." Let's give it a try. Have the children practice a couple of times.

One day a shepherd was out in his field watching his <u>sheep</u>. The shepherd always took good care of his <u>sheep</u>. The shepherd would protect the <u>sheep</u> and keep them in a pen at night. He would make sure they were kept safe. The shepherd would make sure the <u>sheep</u> always had food. Every single one of the <u>sheep</u> was important to the shepherd. The shepherd loved his <u>sheep</u> and took good care of them.

Then one day the shepherd noticed that one little <u>sheep</u> was missing. What do you think the shepherd did? That's right, the shepherd went to look for the missing little <u>sheep</u>. The shepherd looked high and low. The shepherd looked everywhere for the little <u>sheep</u>. The shepherd finally found the lost <u>sheep</u>, and he was so happy.

Do you know why this Bible story is so special? Because it tells us how much God loves us. God is like the shepherd, and you are like the little <u>sheep</u>. You are very important to God. God loves you and takes care of you like the shepherd takes care of his <u>sheep</u>. You are precious to God, and you can trust God to take care of you, because you are his little <u>sheep</u>.

- **Who takes care of and loves his sheep?** *(the shepherd)*
- **Who is precious to God?** *(I am, you are, we are)*
- **Who loves and takes care of you?** *(God)*

Send'em-Off

* Five cotton balls
* Cotton balls
* Completed *Hold'em-Up* for each child

Prayer

Put out five cotton balls to represent sheep. Ask the children to help think of five ways Jesus takes care of us. Then put the cotton balls in your hands as you lead the children in this prayer: **Dear God, thank you for loving and caring for us. Thank you for all you do for us. Thank you for being our Good Shepherd. In Jesus' name, amen.**

Cleanup

Gather the children together. Ask them to pretend to be little sheep as they clean. Then send them out. As their good shepherd, give attention to each one, saying, **I see, (name) the happy little lamb, is making our room neat and clean.**

Homeward Bound

As the children leave, make sure they have their completed *Hold'em-Ups* they made for Bible Story Time. Give each one a cotton ball while telling them it reminds us of sheep, and how they are precious to their shepherd, just like we are precious to Jesus.

* **What does the cotton ball remind you of?**
* **How do you know you are precious to God?**

Home Connections

It's a Snap!

Title: The Good Shepherd

Bible Story: The Lost Sheep *Luke 15:1–7*

Bible Truth: You are precious to God.

Bible Verse: He takes good care of those who trust in him. (Nahum 1:7b)

- In this lesson, your child **heard** how the shepherd searched for his lost lamb because there is nothing more precious to a shepherd than his lambs.

- In this lesson, your child **learned** that he is precious to God, just as a lamb is precious to a shepherd.

- In this lesson, your child **remembered** that God will take good care of those who put their trust in him. Your child can trust God because he or she is valuable to him.

We are precious to God, just as sheep are precious to their shepherd. God loves us and wants the best for us. He loves us so much that if we were lost, he would drop everything to search for us. Instill in your child how much God values and loves your little lamb.

Home Connection

These are items that were used during the Bible story lesson that might be commonly found in your home. When your child sees or plays with one of the items mentioned below, help make the connection to the Bible story.

Sheep: Although you might not have sheep lying around your house, you may have an opportunity to take your child to a petting zoo to see sheep. Or you can look at animal picture books. Anytime you might encounter sheep, remind your child how God is like our shepherd and we are like sheep. God loves us and cares for us; he is the Good Shepherd.

Cotton balls: Cotton balls were used throughout the lesson as reminders of sheep. Whenever you are using cotton balls at home, remind your child of the sheep. Talk about how God is the Good Shepherd who loves and cares for us, his sheep.

Keeping Connected

Here are two simple activities that were used in class during the Bible story lesson of The Good Shepherd. Use these activities to help your child remember the Bible story lesson.

Prayer
Count out five cotton balls to represent sheep and for each one name a way Jesus cares for us. Then put the cotton balls in your hands as you lead your child in this prayer: **Dear God, thank you for loving and caring for us. Thank you for all you do for us. Thank you for being our Good Shepherd. In Jesus' name, amen.**

Little Lambs
Put out pretzel sticks plus large and small marshmallows. Use the food to make little lambs in a sheep pen. Talk about how shepherds take care of their little lambs.

The Butterfly in the Garden

(Easter)

BIBLE STORY:
Jesus' Resurrection
Luke 24

BIBLE TRUTH:
Jesus is alive.

BIBLE VERSE:
Jesus is not here!
He has risen!
(Luke 24:6a)

Imagine the joy of discovering that someone you loved and was dead is now alive! The death and resurrection of our Savior is a complicated concept for young children to grasp, yet is foundational to the Christian faith. Introduce the Bible story concepts and focus on delivering the joyful message that Jesus is alive today!

★ In this lesson, children will **hear** the story of the death and resurrection of Jesus our Savior.

★ In this lesson, children will **learn** that Jesus did not stay dead; he is alive and well today!

★ In this lesson, children will **remember** Jesus did not stay dead but has risen from the dead and is alive.

Lesson Thirteen Snapshot

Get List:

- [ ] 1 copy of the *Hold'em-Up* reproducible (page 106) for each child
- [ ] Scissors
- [ ] Crayons and markers
- [ ] Masking tape
- [ ] CD player
- [ ] CD of Easter music
- [ ] 2 baskets
- [ ] Plastic eggs
- [ ] Building blocks and other construction materials

- [ ] Index cards
- [ ] Glue
- [ ] Round cereal
- [ ] Bowl
- [ ] Bible
- [ ] Paper plates
- [ ] Doughnut holes
- [ ] Small rock, more than two inches in diameter, for each child
- [ ] 1 copy of *Home Connections* (page 111) for each child

The Heart of the Story:

The Easter story is about the joy we find because Jesus is alive. As you teach, be aware of the lasting impact you will have as you lay the foundation of faith in the lives of your children. Do not underestimate the impact teaching children will have. It may seem sometimes like a simple and somewhat insignificant hour or two, but it's not. As the women who tended Jesus' grave were consistent, they were the first to know of the resurrection of Jesus, a story still told after 2,000 years. Enjoy and be filled with joy as you teach your little ones about the amazement found in Jesus who is alive!

Hold'em-Up
Bible Story Reproducible Page

* 1 copy of the reproducible on this page for each child
* Scissors
* Crayons or markers

Copy and cut out the butterfly figure for each child. Have the children color the butterfly. Then fold the middle part in. The children will hold the middle part so the wings will flap when moved up and down.

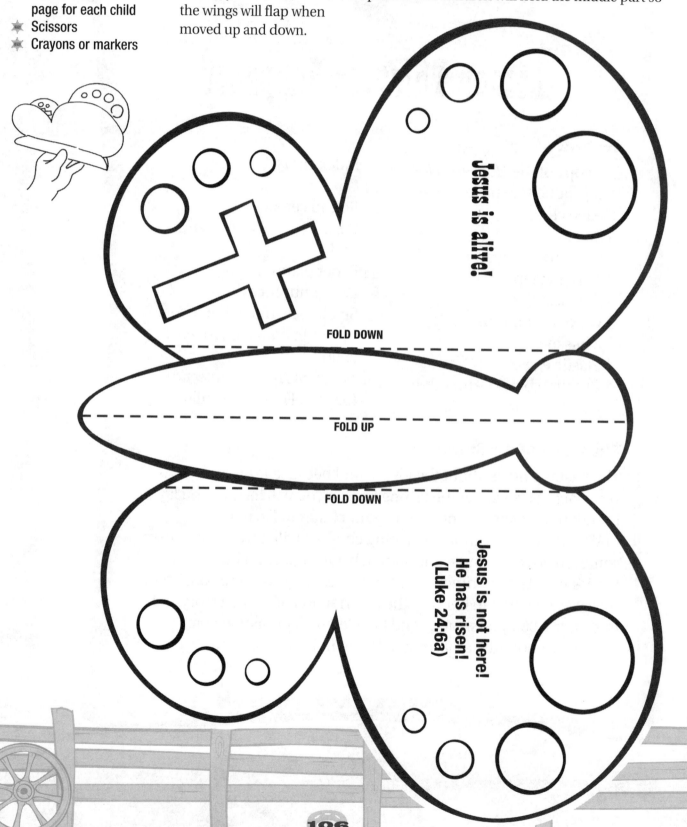

Jesus is alive!

FOLD DOWN

FOLD UP

FOLD DOWN

Jesus is not here!
He has risen!
(Luke 24:6a)

Round'em-Up

Use the *Round'em-Up* activities to gather the children or anytime you need a quick group activity for a transition or filler.

Bible Story Link

- ✹ Masking tape
- ✹ CD player
- ✹ CD of Easter music

Jesus Is Alive!

Use masking tape to mark a large cross on the floor. When you start the music, shout out, **Jesus is alive!** and have the children flitter around the room like butterflies. After a brief segment, stop the music and say, **Jesus died on the cross.** Have the children find a place to stand on the cross. Repeat several times.

Game

- ✹ 2 baskets
- ✹ Plastic eggs

Pass It On!

Put a basket of plastic eggs at one end of the room. Place an empty basket at the other end of the room. Line up the children between the two baskets. Tell the first child in line to pick up an egg from the basket and pass it down the line toward the empty basket. As each person passes the egg they say, "Jesus is alive." Time the children to see how long it takes them to fill the empty basket.

Song/ Fingerplay

Jesus Christ Has Risen

Sing the following words to the tune "If You're Happy and You Know It."

Jesus Christ has risen. Praise the Lord!
(clap your hands and repeat one time)
Jesus Christ has risen!
He has risen from the dead. Oh!
Jesus Christ has risen. Praise the Lord!
(clap your hands)

If you're joyful and you know it,
clap your hands. (repeat one time)
If you're joyful and you know it,
then your face will surely show it.
If you're joyful and you know it,
clap your hands.

Show Me

Butterfly

Have the children show you how they can be butterflies. They can show you a little butterfly and a big butterfly. They can fly like a slow butterfly and a fast butterfly. Have them show you a butterfly that is excited. Tell the exciting news that Jesus is alive!

Bible Story
Hands-on Activities

These activities work well for large or small groups of children, or as stations, to introduce and/or reinforce the Bible story.

Build a Cross

Put out blocks and other building materials for the children to construct crosses. Talk about how Jesus died on a cross, but that the cross is now empty because Jesus rose again and he lives.

* Building blocks and other construction materials

Bible Memory

Jesus is not here! He has risen! (Luke 24:6a)

* Bible

Show the children where to find Luke 24:6 in the Bible. Read it aloud from your Bible. Then sing the following lyrics that include the verse to the tune of "Where is Thumbkin?"

> *Where is Jesus? Where is Jesus?*
> *He's not here, he's not here.*
> *He has risen from the dead.*
> *He's alive just like he said.*
> *He's alive. He's alive!*

The Stone Cross

Before class, cut cross shapes from index cards. Place cereal into a bowl. Talk about how Jesus died on the cross but then rose again. Give each child a cross and show them how to glue the cereal onto the cross with little drops of glue. Tell them we know Jesus is alive because the stone was rolled away. Explain how the round cereal reminds us of the stone that was rolled away.

* Index cards
* Scissors
* Glue
* Round cereal
* Bowl

Roll the Stone Away

Before class, cut a one-inch hole in the center of several paper plates. Talk about how the doughnuts remind you of the stone that was rolled away, because Jesus was alive. Have the children place a doughnut hole on their plate. (Place another plate underneath to catch the doughnut hole.) Have them roll the doughnut hole around the plate trying to make it roll into the hole. When it does, have the children shout, "Roll the stone away. Jesus is alive today!" *Note: Check with parents for any food allergies children may have.*

* Paper plates
* Scissors
* Doughnut holes

Bible Story Time

* Bible
* Completed *Hold'em-Up* (made from page 106) for each child

Gather your children for Story Time; be sure all the children have their *Hold'em-Ups* ready to go. **You're going to help me tell our Bible story today. Everyone show me your butterflies.** Have the children hold their butterflies so the wings will flap freely. **When I point to you, flap your butterflies and say, "Jesus is not here; he has risen!"** Point to the children for practice.

Seeing your little butterflies reminds me of our Bible story. Hold up a Bible for the children to see. **Our Bible story is found in the book of Luke. I'm going to tell you that story but just for fun include how a pretend butterfly might have watched it happen.**

One day a little butterfly was sitting on a branch as he saw Jesus die on a cross. This made the little butterfly very sad. Later, the little butterfly flew to a special garden where he sat on a different branch and saw some people put Jesus' body in a tomb. Then they rolled a big round stone to cover the opening of the tomb.

Three days later, the little butterfly was back at that same garden. But this time, the butterfly happened to land on a very large stone. It was the stone that covered the opening to the tomb where the people put Jesus' body. While the butterfly was sitting on the stone, there was an earthquake and the stone began to roll. The butterfly took flight and watched as the stone rolled away from the opening to the tomb where the people had put Jesus three days ago.

The little butterfly flew inside the tomb and looked but did not see Jesus. Where was Jesus? Point. **The little butterfly was so happy that it wanted to shout ...** point. **Of course we know butterflies can't shout.**

Soon the butterfly saw some women come into the garden going toward the empty tomb. The women were sad because they did not know that Jesus was alive. The little butterfly landed on the shoulder of one of the ladies and wanted to shout ... (point) **so the women would be happy too. Soon the women saw that the stone was rolled away. They were so surprised. They were very happy because now they knew that ...** (point).

* **Who has risen?** *(Jesus)*
* **Why were the women happy?** *(Jesus was not in the tomb, he had risen)*
* **Who is alive today?** *(Jesus)*

Send'em-Off

- Small rock more than two inches in diameter per child
- Completed *Hold'em-Up* for each child

Teacher Tip

Children are susceptible to choking hazards. Please use a choke tube when trying to decide whether a stone may be too small for children to handle.

Itty Bitty Bible Facts

Women typically visited a grave to place perfume on the body. It was a custom that honored the life and memory of the one who died and was a part of the grieving process for people of the time. The women's plan was interrupted by the shocking realization that Jesus' body was not in the tomb.

Prayer

There is so much to be joyful for. Have the children talk about things that make them joyful. Let's give Jesus a little prayerful shout-out for joy. Here is a cheer to show how joyful we are.

Give me a J. Have the children echo "J"; continue to spell out the rest of "Jesus."

What's that spell? Have the children say "Jesus."

Louder! Children echo "Jesus." **Louder!** Echo "Jesus."

Jesus, Jesus, thank you Jesus. Thank you for the joy you give. Have the children repeat.

Cleanup

Get those joyful jumpers ready to clean up. Have the children jump for joy on your command. Say, **Everyone who is joyful jump ___** (call out a number between one and four) **times.** Then have all the children pick up one item. When everyone has picked up one item, say it again and select a different number. Continue until the room is all picked up.

Homeward Bound

As the children leave, make sure they have their completed *Hold'em-Ups* they made for Bible Story Time. Hand each child a rock that is at least two-inches in diameter so it does not present a choking hazard. Tell the children this rock will remind them of the stone in the Bible story that was rolled away. Then have the children repeat after you, "Rock 'n' roll the stone away. Jesus is alive today!"

- **What makes you happy?**
- **What does your rock remind you of?**

Home Connections

It's a Snap!

Title: The Butterfly in the Garden (Easter)

Bible Story: Jesus' Resurrection *Luke 24*

Bible Truth: Jesus is alive.

Bible Verse: Jesus is not here! He has risen! (Luke 24:6a)

- In this lesson, your child **heard** the story of the death and resurrection of Jesus our Savior.

- In this lesson, your child **learned** that Jesus did not stay dead; he is alive and well today!

- In this lesson, your child **remembered** Jesus did not stay dead but has risen from the dead and is alive.

The resurrection is the means for the forgiveness of our sins, because Jesus became the ultimate sacrifice. We can live with Jesus for eternity, because he rose in victory over death. So were the people excited to see that Jesus had indeed risen from the dead? They were ecstatic. They were filled with joy. Share that joy with your little one by celebrating the resurrection of our Savior.

Home Connection

These are items that were used during the Bible story lesson that might be commonly found in your home. When your child sees or plays with one of the items mentioned below, help make the connection to the Bible story.

Butterfly: Whenever you see a butterfly, remind your child of the resurrection of Jesus. Talk about how Jesus died but rose again. Remind him or her of the Bible story told by the little butterfly—Jesus is alive!

Plastic eggs: Plastic eggs can be a reminder of how the stone was rolled away on Easter morning. Have fun with your child as he rolls plastic eggs across your floor. Jesus is not dead; he is alive.

Keeping Connected

Here are two simple activities that were used in class during the Bible story lesson of Jesus' resurrection. Use these activities to help your child remember the Bible story lesson.

Jesus Christ Has Risen (*Song/Finger Play*)
Sing to the tune of "Where is Thumbkin?"

Where is Jesus? Where is Jesus? He's not here. He's not here.
He has risen from the dead. He's alive just like he said.
He's alive. He's alive!

Build a cross
Collect building blocks, small empty boxes and other materials you can use to build a cross. Talk about how Jesus died on a cross but that the cross is now empty because Jesus rose again and he lives.

Topic Index

Scripture Index